Advanced Stories for Reproduction

First Series

L. A. HILL

Oxford University Press
外 國 語 研 修 社

Oxford University Press, Walton Street, Oxford OX2 6DP
OXFORD LONDON GLASGOW
NEW YORK TORONTO MELBOURNE WELLINGTON
KUALA LUMPUR SINGAPORE HONG KONG TOKYO
DELHI BOMBAY CALCUTTA MADRAS KARACHI
NAIROBI DAR ES SALAAM CAPE TOWN

ISBN 0 19 432543 1

© OXFORD UNIVERSITY PRESS, 1965

First published 1965
Reprinted 1966
Reset and reprinted 1968
Ninth impression 1980

First Korean impression 1985

Illustrated by DENNIS MALLET, MSIA

영어의 표현력 및 이해력 양성에 역점을 둔 L.A.HILL 박사의
명저 Stories for Reproduction 총서 한국판을 내놓으면서

우리의 국력이 크게 신장되어 국제 교류의 폭이 확대되어 감에 따라 각계 각층에서 영어에 능통한 인재의 요구가 날로 늘어가고 있읍니다. 그러나 이러한 실력을 갖춘 인재는 구하기가 쉽지 않을 뿐 아니라, 최고 학부를 나온 분들 마저 영어를 필요로 하는 업무에 부닥치면 **표현력**(말과 글로 표현하기)이나 이해력(읽거나 듣고 이해하기) 부족 때문에 많은 곤란을 겪고 있읍니다.

따지고 보면 이러한 현상이 생기게 된 것은 당연한 결과라고 할 수 있겠읍니다. 왜냐하면 지금까지의 영어 교육이 난해한 영문의 국역이나 까다로운 문법체계의 학습에 치중한 나머지 **작문력, 회화력, 독해력** 특히 **속독력** 및 **청해력** 등을 양성하는 학습을 소홀히 해 왔기 때문입니다.

그렇다면 영어의 **표현력**과 이해력을 기르기 위해서는 무엇부터 시작하여 어떻게 해야 하는지 그 구체적인 방법을 살펴 보기로 합시다.

1. 상용 2000 단어의 철저한 학습과 활용

영어로 일상적인 의사표시를 하는 데 있어서는 빈도수가 높은 것만을 뽑아 만든 **2,000 상용 단어**만의 사용으로 부족함이 없읍니다. 예를 들면 **6만**의 표제어와 **6만 9천**의 예문을 싣고 있는 **Longman Dictionary of Contemporary English**는 표제어의 정의와 그 예문을 제시하는 데 **2,000**의 「**정의 어휘**(Defining Vocabulary)」와 단순한 문법구조만을 쓰고 있으며, **Longman Dictionary of Business English**도 Michael West의 상용 영어 단어 일람표(A General Service List of English Words)를 토대로 한 2,000여 단어와 단순한 문법구조만으로 Business 각 분야의 **전문용어**를 완벽하게 해설하고 있읍니다.

이런 사실만을 보아도 영어 실력 양성에 있어서 **2,000**상용 단어의 **철저한** 학습과 그 활용연습이 얼마나 중요한 것이라는 것을 쉽게 이해할 수 있을 것입니다.

그럼에도 불구하고 이 **2,000**상용 단어의 철저한 기초학습이 채 끝나기도 전에, 일상적 의사표시에는 별로 쓰이지 않아 기억하기도 힘든 많은 어려운 영어 단어들(고교 수준에서는 약 **5,000**, 대학과 대학원 수준에서는 **10,000~30,000**단어)을 단편적, 기계적으로 암기하거나 난해한 영문의 국역이나 까다로운 문법체계의 학습에만 매달린다면 아무리 노력을 해 봤자 모래 위에 성을 쌓는 격이어서, 영어로 자신의 생각을 **자유롭게 표현**할 수 있는 정도까지 그 실력이 향상되기를 기대할 수 없는 것입니다.

2. 문맥적 접근법(Contextualized Approach)

어학의 습득은 「의미내용」의 「기억, 재현」과정을 통해 이루어지는 것이며, 이 「의미내용」을 전달하는 효율은 1. 숫자(Figure) 2. 문자(Letter) 3. 단어(Word) 4. 문(Sentence) 5. 문장의 절(Paragraph)순으로, 그것이 함축하는 「의미내용」의 차원이 높은 것일수록 그 전달량이 커지고 전달 효율이 높아집니다. 따라서 영어 학습에 있어서도 단어나 문법을 따로 학습하는 것보다는 문장내에서 문맥(Context)에 따라 이를 학습하는 것이 그 기억과 재현의 효율을 높일 수 있는 것입니다.

3. 표현력 향상을 위한 재현(Reproduction)연습

영어의 표현력을 기르는 데는 모범적인 영어 문장을 되풀이해서 읽고 이것을 재현(Reproduction)하는 연습을 해 보는 것이 가장 효과적이라는 것은 이미 널리 알려진 사실입니다. 그래서 중·고교의 교과서를 한 권이라도 암기해 보라고 권유하는 분들이 많으나, 이 교과서 자체가 암기와 재현 연습용으로 쓰기에는, 본문의 길이가 너무 길거나 난해할 뿐 아니라 재현 연습을 유도하는 적절한 Questions, Exercises 및 Answer Key 등의 뒷받침이 되어 있지 않기 때문에 표현력 향상을 위한 교재로는 적합하지 못합니다.

영어 교육계의 오랜 경험에서 밝혀진 바에 의하면 표현력 양성을 목적으로 하는 영어 문장 재현 연습용의 교재는 다음과 같은 요건을 갖춘 것이 가장 효과가 높다는 것입니다.

첫째 교재 본문의 내용이 학습자의 지속적인 흥미와 관심을 끌 수 있을 만큼 재미 있으면서도 교육적 가치가 풍부한 것이어야 하며,

둘째 교재에 사용되는 단어, 숙어, 문법구조등이 각 학습단계(입문, 초급, 중급, 상급수준 등)에 꼭 알맞게 제한 사용되어야 하며,

셋째 재현 연습에 쓰일 본문의 길이도 기억과 재현에 알맞는 단어수(학습 단계에 따라 150 단어 내지 350 단어의 길이)를 초과하지 않아야 하고,

넷째 학습시키고자 하는 단어, 숙어, 문법구조등이 교재의 본문에 흡수·통합되어 이것들이 각기 따로 따로 유리되어 있을 때보다 높은 차원의 「의미내용」을 갖도록 하여야 한다는 것입니다.

따라서 영어의 표현력과 이해력의 종합적인 향상을 위해서는 무엇보다 먼저 위에 열거한 네가지 요건을 갖춘 교재가 절대 필요한 것입니다. 그런데 이러한 교재의 입수가 지극히 어렵던 차에, 다행히 옥스포드대학출판부에서, 이 방면의 세계적 권위자인 L.A.HILL 박사로 하여금 위에 적은 네가지 요건을 모두 갖춘 영어 학습교재 총서를 저술케하여, 이를 최근에 모두 펴 내놓아 외국어로서 영어를 배우는 전세계 영어학도들의 절

찬을 받고 있는 것을 보고, 실용 영어의 통신교육과 그에 부수되는 영어 교재의 **출판**을 전문으로 하고 있는 저희 外國語研修社에서는, 이 교재의 한국내 출판이 저희들의 사업목적에 부합될 뿐 아니라 이러한 교재를 찾고 있는 수 많은 독자와 영어 교사들에게 크게 도움이 되리라고 생각하고 작년부터 옥스포드대학출판부와 판권 교섭을 해 오던 끝에 금년들어 계약이 성립되어 **L. A. HILL**박사 저술의 영어 학습 교재중 **표현력 및 이해력** 향상에 역점을 둔 교재 전 **4**집을 아래와 같이 내놓게 되었습니다.

제 1 집 **Stories for Reproduction 1**: 입문편, 초급편, 중급편 및 상급편의 Text 각 1 권과 그 Study Guide(학습안내서)각 1 권 및 이에 딸린 음성교재용 녹음테이프.

제 2 집 **Stories for Reproduction 2** : 입문편, 초급편, 중급편 및 상급편의 Text 각 1 권과 그 Answer Key 각 1 권 및 이에 딸린 음성교재용 녹음테이프.

제 3 집 **Steps to Understanding**: 입문편, 초급편, 중급편 및 상급편의 Text 각 1 권 과 그 Answer Key 각 1 권 및 이에 딸린 음성교재용 녹음테이프.

제 4 집 **Stories for Reproduction (American Series)** : 초급편, 중급편 및 상급편의 Text 각 1 권과 그 Answer Key 및 이에 딸린 음성교재용 녹음테이프.

전 세계적인 Best Seller 가 되어 있는 이 교재는 표현력과 독해력 향상에 필수적인 단어·숙어와 문법구조를 4 단계로 나누어 제한 사용하고 있어 독자들에게 학습상의 부담을 주지 않을 뿐 아니라 그 본문이 유우머(해학)와 윗트(기지)로 가득찬 흥미진진한 짧은 이야기로 되어 있기 때문에 그것을 끝까지 단숨에 읽을 수 있도록 되어 있으며, 이 이야기를 **속독**, **청취**, **정독**, **재청**(再聽)한 다음 다양한 **Questions**와 **Exercises** 를 사용한 문답식 방법으로 그 내용을 이해하는 훈련을 쌓는 동시에 이를 다시 말과 글로 표현해 보는(**Oral & Written Reproduction**)연습을 되풀이 함으로써, 난해한 영문국역, 단편적인 단어·숙어의 암기나 문법체계의 학습등에서 오는 정신적 긴장과 피로를 수반하지 않고, 독자들이 이야기의 내용을 즐기다 보면 자기도 모르는 사이에 이해력과 표현력이 몸에 붙도록 꾸며져 있습니다.

또한 이 교재는 Text와는 따로 **Study Guide**(학습안내서), **Answer Key** (해답집) 및 녹음테이프가 딸려 있어 개인의 자습(Self-Study)용으로는 물론 교실 수업용으로도 쓸 수 있도록 만들어져 있습니다.

이 교재가 많은 독자들의 영어 표현력 및 이해력 향상에 획기적인 도움이 되기를 바랍니다.

1985년 1월 5일

外國語研修社

代表理事
會 長 李 瀅 載

머 리 말

이 책은 재미 있고 읽기 쉬운 이야기를 사용하여 영어의 **이해력**(읽거나 듣고 이해하기)과 **표현력**(말이나 글로 나타내기)을 향상시킬 것을 목적으로 하고 있습니다.

이 책은 그 상급편입니다. 중급편을 마친 분은 이 책을 이용하여 한 층 더 높은 영어 실력을 쌓을 수 있도록 꾸며져 있습니다.

구성

이 책에는 225~350 단어 길이로 쓰여진 이야기 60 편이 담겨져 있으며 각 편마다 이야기의 내용을 말이나 글로 재현(**Oral or Written Reproduction**)하는 공부를 시키기 위한 질의문과 그 해답이 **Study Guide** (주해서)에 따로 실려 있습니다.

이 책의 본문으로 쓰여진 이야기는 권말의 부록에 수록된 2,075단어의 범위 안에서 쓰여진 평이한 것이며 문법구조는 A. S. Hornby의 A Guide to Patterns and Usage in English에 따랐으므로 중급편보다는 약간 그 정도가 높으나 중급편을 마친 분이나 동등 이상의 영어 실력이면 충분히 이해할 수 있는 구조로 되어 있습니다.

Study Guide 와 음성교재

이 책에는 지도교사 없이 혼자서 자습하는 분들의 학습을 돕기 위하여 따로 Study Guide (주해서)가 마련되어 있습니다. 이 Study Guide는 (1) 본문에 나오는 중요한 단어·숙어의 뜻, 발음 및 어법의 상세한 해설과 그 예문으로 이루어진 **Notes,** (2) 이야기의 요점을 적어 놓은 **Point of the Story,** (3)재현 연습에 알맞게 만들어진 **Questions** 와 (4) 질의문에 대한 해답(**Answer Key**)으로 구성되어 있습니다.

이 교재에 딸려있는 음성교재는 교양 있는 영국의 일류 성우가 표준영어를 사용하여 취입한 것으로 이야기 전문(全文)과 그 내용의 질의문이 재현 연습에 꼭 알맞도록 녹음되어있어 영어의 청취력 및 회화력 향상을 위해서는 더할 나위 없이 적합한 교재입니다.

공부하는 방법

(1) **혼자서 자습하는 경우** 가정에서 지도교사 없이 자습하는 경우에는 먼저 녹음테이프로 본문의 이야기를 1~2회 들은 다음 책을 펴 보고 얼마나 정확하게 알아들었는지 확인해 봅니다. 만일 새로운 단어·숙어나 표현법이 있어 확실한 이해가 되지 않으면 Study Guide를 펴서 Notes를 참조하고 그래도 미심쩍으면 사전을 찾아 봅니다. 청해력에 자신이 없는 분들은 먼저 본문을 2~3회 읽고 난 후 대충 이해가 된 다음에 녹음테이프를 들어도 좋습니다. 이야기의 내용이 이해가 되면 이번에는 책을 덮고 그 내용을 되도록 많이 공책에 써서 재현해 본 다음 원문과 비교하여 틀린 곳을 바로잡아 가는

것이 대단히 중요합니다.

　Study Guide에 이야기의 내용을 순서대로 조금씩 재현시키기 위한 질문이 각 편마다 수록되어 있습니다. 이 질문에 대한 답을 완전한 문장 형식으로 공책에 써 본 후 Study Guide 말미에 실려 있는 Answer Key와 대조해 보고 틀린 점을 바로잡습니다. 그 다음에는 테이프로 이야기를 2～3회 다시 들어 보고 질문을 들으면서 구두로 답을 해 본 후 Study Guide의 정답과 대조해 봅니다.

　(2) 교실수업에 이용하는 경우 교실수업의 경우에는 이 교재를 다음과 같은 방법으로 이용할 수 있겠습니다.

　(i) 청취 후 구두 발표(Listening and Speaking)

　선생이 학생들에게 이야기를 2～3회 낭독해 주거나 녹음된 테이프로 이야기를 2～3회 들려 준 다음 그 내용을 구두로 재현하도록 하거나 Study Guide에 나오는 질문에 구두로 답변하도록 합니다. 이 방법은 30인 이내의 적은 인원수일 경우에 가장 적합합니다.

　(ii) 청취 후 다시 써 보기(Listening and Writing)

　선생님이 학생들에게 이야기를 2～3회 낭독해 주거나 녹음된 테이프로 들려 준 다음 기억해 낼 수 있는 최대한으로 이야기의 내용을 공책에 써 보도록 합니다. 그 다음에는 Study Guide에 있는 질문들을 받아쓰게 하거나 칠판에 써 놓고 그 답을 공책에 써 보도록 합니다. 이 방법은 학생수가 50인 내외인 교실수업의 경우에 적합합니다.

　(iii) 읽은 후 다시 써 보기(Reading and Writing)

　학생들로 하여금 이야기를 되도록 빠른 속도로 읽게 한 후 간단한 True or False Questions를 만들어 속독력을 평가해 봅니다. 다음에는 이야기를 2～3회 정독시킨 후 책을 덮고 이야기를 최대한으로 기억하여 공책에 써 보도록 하거나 질문들에 대한 답을 공책에 써 보도록 합니다.

　(i) (ii) (iii) 어느 경우에나 이야기를 읽거나 듣는 것과 그 재현 사이에 며칠간의 간격을 두는 것이 경우에 따라서는 더욱 효과적일 수도 있습니다.

　L. A. Hill 박사가 2,075표제어 수준으로 쓴 교재에는 다음과 같은 것들이 있습니다.

Word Power 4500: Vocabulary Tests and Exercises in American English

Advanced Stories for Reproduction, Series 2

Advanced Stories for Reproduction, American Series

Advanced Steps to Understanding

Oxford Graded Readers, 2075-Headword Level: Junior and Senior Stories

Introduction

This is the third in a series of stories for reproduction which begins with *Elementary Stories for Reproduction* and continues with *Intermediate Stories for Reproduction*. A fourth book, *Note-taking Practice*, provides students with training in note-taking at lectures.

This book contains 60 stories, each between 225 and 350 words long, and all written within the 2,075-word vocabulary given in the Appendix. The grammatical patterns are limited to those in A. S. Hornby's *A Guide to Patterns and Usage in English*.

Here are some ways in which the stories in this book can be used:

1. *Listening and Speaking*

Only the teacher has the book. He reads one of the stories aloud to the students two or three times, and they then have to retell the story orally, or to answer oral questions about it. This is best done in very small classes, of course.

2. *Listening and Writing*

Only the teacher has the book. He reads one of the stories to the students two or three times, and they then write down as much of it as they can remember, or answer questions about it in writing (the questions can be written on the blackboard, or dictated by the teacher). This can be done in a large class.

3. *Reading and Writing*

Each student has a copy of the book. He reads one of the stories for a certain number of minutes, then shuts the book and writes down as much of the story as he can remember, or answers questions about it in writing. The questions can be written on the blackboard, or dictated by the teacher.

With 1, 2, and 3, there can be an interval of time—even of several days—between the telling of the story and the reproduction.

3 can be done by students who have no teacher. They can read a story, close their books and then write down as much of the story as they can remember. When they have finished, they can open their books again and check what they have written by referring to the story in the book.

Advanced Stories for Reproduction

First Series

1

As one approaches *some* crossroads, one comes to a sign which says that drivers have to stop when they come to the main road ahead. At other crossroads, drivers have to go slow, but they do not actually have to stop (unless, of course, there is something coming along the main road); and at still others, they do not have either to stop or to go slow, because they are themselves on the main road.

Mr Williams, who was always a very careful driver, was driving home from work one evening when he came to a crossroads. It had a 'Slow' sign, so he slowed down when he came to the main road, looked both ways to see that nothing was coming, and then drove across without stopping completely.

At once he heard a police whistle, so he pulled in to the side of the road and stopped. A policeman walked over to him with a notebook and pencil in his hand and said, 'You didn't stop at that crossing.'

'But the sign there doesn't say "Stop",' answered Mr Williams. 'It just says "Slow", and I *did* go slow.'

The policeman looked around him, and a look of surprise came over his face. Then he put his notebook and pencil away, scratched his head and said, 'Well, I'll be blowed! I am in the wrong street!'

2

Before the last war, officers in the navy had a lot more freedom when their ship was in port than they have nowadays. They were expected to lead a busy social life, and to take an active part in sport ashore. It was therefore rather difficult for them to find time to do all their other duties.

Usually, all the officers in a ship used to have a regular meeting together once a week to receive orders from their captain, make reports and discuss any business that had to be discussed, such as who should represent the ship in the next football match.

One such meeting was being held on board a ship one day, and after the regular business had been completed, the time came to discuss the date of the next meeting. Friday of the next week was suggested, and so was Monday of the week after, but both of them interfered with somebody's arrangements for the weekend, and in the end it was generally agreed that the meeting should be held on Wednesday, as this would be the least likely day to interfere with anybody's convenience, since it was right in the middle of the week.

As the officers were leaving, however, one of them was heard to say, 'Wednesday is the *worst* day, because it interferes with *two* weekends!'

3

Mr and Mrs Williams had always spent their summer holidays in England in the past, in a small boarding-house at the seaside. One year, however, Mr Williams made a lot of money in his business, so they decided to go to Rome and stay at a really good hotel while they went around and saw the sights of that famous city.

They flew to Rome, and arrived at their hotel late one evening. They expected that they would have to go to bed hungry, because in the boarding-houses they had been used to in the past, no meals were served after seven o'clock in the evening. They were therefore surprised when the clerk who received them in the hall of the hotel asked them whether they would be taking dinner there that night.

'Are you still serving dinner then?' asked Mrs Williams.

'Yes, certainly, madam,' answered the clerk. 'We serve it until half-past nine.'

'What are the times of meals then?' asked Mr Williams.

'Well, sir,' answered the clerk, 'we serve breakfast from seven to half-past eleven in the morning, lunch from twelve to three in the afternoon, tea from four to five, and dinner from six to half-past nine.'

'But that hardly leaves any time for us to see the sights of Rome!' said Mrs Williams in a disappointed voice.

4

Mrs Black was having a lot of trouble with her skin, so she went to her doctor about it. He could not find anything wrong with her, however, so he sent her to the local hospital for some tests. The hospital, of course, sent the results of the tests direct to Mrs Black's doctor, and the next morning he telephoned her to give her a list of the things that he thought she should not eat, as any of them might be the cause of her skin trouble.

Mrs Black carefully wrote all the things down on a piece of paper, which she then left beside the telephone while she went out to a ladies' meeting.

When she got back home two hours later, she found her husband waiting for her. He had a big basket full of packages beside him, and when he saw her, he said, 'Hullo, dear. I have done all your shopping for you.'

'Done all my shopping?' she asked in surprise. 'But how did you know what I wanted?'

'Well, when I got home, I found your shopping list beside the telephone,' answered her husband, 'so I went down to the shops and bought everything you had written down.'

Of course, Mrs Black had to tell him that he had bought all the things the doctor did not allow her to .eat!

5

Some young soldiers who had recently joined the army were being trained in modern ways of fighting, and one of the things they were shown was how an unarmed man could trick an armed enemy and take his weapon away from him. First one of their two instructors took a knife away from the other, using only his bare hands; and then he took a rifle away from him in the same way.

After the lesson, and before they went on to train the young soldiers to do these things themselves, the two instructors asked them a number of questions to see how well they had understood what they had been shown. One of the questions was this: 'Well, you now know what an unarmed man can do against a man with a rifle. Imagine that you are guarding a bridge at night, and that you have a rifle. Suddenly you see an unarmed enemy soldier coming towards you. What will you do?'

The young soldier who had to answer this question thought carefully for a few seconds before he answered, and then said, 'Well, after what I have just seen, I think that the first thing I would do would be to get rid of my rifle as quickly as I could so that the unarmed enemy soldier couldn't take it from me and kill me with it!'

6

A certain poet had written a play, and arrangements were being made to perform it. Of course, the poet was asked to give his advice on the scenery, the lighting, and all the other things that help to make a play successful, and he proved to be a very difficult man to please, as he had his own very definite ideas of how each scene should look.

In one of the scenes in the play, it was necessary to produce the effect of a wonderful sunset, which the young lovers watched together before singing one of their great love songs.

The theatre electricians worked very hard to produce this sunset effect. They tried out all kinds of arrangements and combinations of lights—red lights, orange lights, yellow lights, blue lights, lights from above, lights from behind, lights from the front, lights from the sides—but nothing satisfied the poet, until suddenly he saw exactly the effect that he had been dreaming of producing ever since he had written his play.

'That's it!' he shouted excitedly to the electricians behind the stage. 'That's just right! Keep it exactly like that!'

'I'm sorry, sir,' answered the chief electrician, 'but we can't keep it like this.'

'Why ever not?' asked the poet angrily.

'Because the theatre is on fire, sir,' answered the chief electrician. '*That's* what's producing the effect you can see now!'

7

Nasreddin never seemed to have enough money to pay his bills, so he always owed money to the shopkeepers in his town. Most of them were patient, understanding men and did not speak to him very often about the money that he owed them, but there was one who was not at all patient, and who was also very fond of money. Whenever this man saw Nasreddin, he reminded him of the money that he had not yet paid him, and he very often did this in front of Nasreddin's best friends, which made Nasreddin feel very uncomfortable, as he did not want his friends to know that he was so poor.

One day, therefore, Nasreddin decided to teach the shopkeeper a lesson.

The next time that the man stopped him in the street and began to shame him publicly about his debt to him, Nasreddin said, 'Wait a minute. How much money do I in fact owe you?'

'You owe me exactly one hundred and twenty-two liras,' answered the shopkeeper.

'Well,' said Nasreddin, 'if I paid you forty liras this month, another forty next month, and forty more the month after that, how much would I still owe you?'

'You would then owe me two liras, of course,' answered the shopkeeper.

'Well, aren't you ashamed of yourself,' Nasreddin said, 'giving me all this trouble for only two liras?'

8

Mrs Baker's sister was ill. She had someone to look after her from Monday to Friday, but not at the weekend, so every Friday evening Mrs Baker used to go off to spend the weekend with her at her home in a neighbouring town. But as Mr Baker could not cook, she had arranged for *his* sister to come over and spend the weekend looking after him at their home.

This meant that Mr Baker had quite a busy time when he came home from work on Friday evenings. First he had to drive home from the railway station. Then he had to drive his wife to the station to catch her train. And then he had to wait until his sister's train arrived, so as to take her to his house.

Of course, on Sunday evening he had to drive his sister to the station to catch her train back home, and then wait for his wife's train, so as to bring *her* home.

One Sunday evening he had seen his sister off on her train and was waiting for his wife's arrival when a porter, who had often seen him at the station, came over and spoke to him.

'You are having a lot of fun,' he said. 'But one day one of those women is going to catch you with the other, and then you will be in real trouble!'

9

9

A gay young man, who earned his living as a drummer in a band, had just married, and he and his wife were looking for somewhere to live. They saw a lot of places, but there was always something that one of them did not like about them. At last, however, they found a block of new flats which both of them really liked. However, there was still the problem of whether they should take one of the ground-floor flats, which had a small garden, or one of the upstairs ones.

At last they decided on a first-floor flat—not too low down and not too high up—and moved in. After they had bought furniture, carpets, curtains, and all the rest, they gave a big party to celebrate the setting up of their first home together.

It was a gay and noisy party, as all the host's friends from the band came and played their instruments. The guests danced, sang and practised on their host's drums.

Soon after one a.m. the telephone rang. The hostess went to answer it in the hall, and after she had finished, came back with a happy smile on her face and said to her husband, 'That was the man who has just moved into the flat downstairs telephoning, dear. I am so glad we decided not to choose it. He says it is terribly noisy down there.'

10

Just after the last war, people were very willing to give money to help those who had suffered from it. But not everyone who collected money was honest. The newspapers were full of stories of people who had been cheated by men who went from house to house saying that they were collecting for soldiers who had been seriously wounded in the war, or for people who had lost their homes, or for some other noble cause, while all the time they were putting the money they collected into their own pockets instead of using it for the purposes they claimed to be collecting it for.

One day Mr Smith came back with another story of this kind. He told his wife that a group of people had collected thousands of dollars for the widow of the Unknown Soldier. Then someone had written to the papers about it, and they had written articles to warn other people. Mr Smith said that he and his friends at the office had had a good laugh about the story when they had read it in the newspaper.

'Can you imagine anyone being so stupid as to believe that story and give money for the widow of the Unknown Soldier?' he asked his wife.

She looked puzzled at first, but then her face brightened. 'Oh, yes! I see now!' she answered. 'Of course, the *government* pays the widow of the Unknown Soldier!'

11

Mr and Mrs Davies had left their Christmas shopping very late. There were only a few days more before Christmas, and of course the shops and streets were terribly crowded, but they had to get presents for their family and friends, so they started out early one morning for the big city, and spent several tiring hours buying the things they wanted in the big shops.

By lunch-time, Mr Davies was loaded down with parcels of all shapes and sizes. He could hardly see where he was going as he and his wife left the last shop on their way to the railway station and home. Outside the shop they had to cross a busy street, made even busier than usual by the thousands of people who had come by car to do their last-minute Christmas shopping.

Mr and Mrs Davies had to wait for the traffic lights to change, but as Mr Davies could not see in front of him properly, he gradually moved forward into the road without realizing it. Mrs Davies saw this and became worried. Several times she urged her husband to come back off the road, but without success. He could not hear her because of the noise of the traffic.

Finally she shouted in a voice that could be heard clearly above all the noise, 'Henry! If you intend to stand in that dangerous position a moment longer, give *me* the parcels!'

12

Most of Nasreddin's neighbours were pleasant people, who were always ready to help each other when they were in trouble; but there was one woman who lived in his street who was disliked by everybody because she was always interfering in other people's business, and because she was always borrowing things from people and then forgetting to give them back.

Early one morning, Nasreddin heard a knock at his front door, and, when he opened it, found this woman outside.

'Good morning, Nasreddin,' she said. 'I have to take some things to my sister's house in the town today, and I have not got a donkey, as you know. Will you lend me yours? I will bring it back this evening.'

'I am sorry,' answered Nasreddin. 'If my donkey was here, I would of course lend it to you very willingly, but it is not.'

'Oh?' said the woman. 'It was here last night, because I saw it behind your house. Where is it now?'

'My wife took it into town early this morning,' answered Nasreddin.

Just then the donkey brayed loudly.

'You are not telling the truth, Nasreddin!' the woman said angrily. 'I can hear your donkey. You should be ashamed of yourself, telling lies to a neighbour!'

'You are the one who should be ashamed, not me!' shouted Nasreddin. 'Is it good manners to believe a donkey's word rather than that of one of one's neighbours?'

13

Nasreddin had to preach in the mosque every Friday, but he did not like this duty at all, and was always looking for ways to avoid it. One Friday he had a good idea. When he went up to begin to preach to the people in the mosque, he said to them, 'Do you know what I am going to talk to you about?'

They were surprised and answered, 'No, we do not.'

Then Nasreddin said, 'Well, if you do not know anything about such an important matter, it is a waste of time for me to talk to you about it.' And he went down again without preaching to the people.

The next Friday, he again asked the question, 'Do you know what I am going to talk to you about today?'

This time the people thought that they had learnt their lesson, so they all said, 'Yes, we do.'

Then Nasreddin said to them, 'Well, it is a waste of time to tell people things that they already know.' And again he went down without preaching to the people.

The third Friday, Nasreddin again said, 'Do you know what I am going to preach to you about today?', but this time some people answered, 'Yes,' and some answered, 'No.'

'Well,' said Nasreddin, 'if some of you know, and some of you do not, those that *do* can tell those that do not,' and again he went down without saying another word.

14

Late one night, Nasreddin was woken up by a terrible noise in the street outside his house. It sounded as if a terrible fight was going on, and as Nasreddin loved nothing better than to watch a fight in the street, he opened his window and looked out. He saw two young men fighting just outside his front door, but when they saw him watching them, they went round the corner of the house and continued to shout at each other and to hit each other there.

Nasreddin did not want to miss anything, so he ran down and opened his front door, but, as it was a cold night, he wrapped himself in a blanket before he went out.

He walked to the corner of his house and looked round it. The two men were still shouting and struggling. Nasreddin went closer to them, both to see the fight better and to try to find out what the men were fighting about. But as soon as he was within easy reach of the men, they stopped fighting, attacked him, seized his blanket and ran away into the darkness with it.

Nasreddin was too old to run after them, so he could do nothing but go sadly back to bed without his blanket.

'Well,' said his wife. 'What were they fighting about?'

'It seems that they were fighting about my blanket,' answered Nasreddin, 'because as soon as they got it, their quarrel ended.'

15

Mr and Mrs Jones's flat was full of suitcases, trunks and packed-up furniture. The two of them were busy with pencils and paper, checking their lists of luggage, when there was a ring at the door. Mrs Jones went to open it, and saw a well-dressed middle-aged lady outside. The lady said that she lived in the flat beside theirs, and that she had come to welcome them to their new home.

The Joneses invited her in, after apologizing for the state of the flat.

'Oh, please don't stand on ceremony with me,' she answered. 'Do you know, in some parts of this town neighbours are not at all friendly. There are some streets—and even some blocks of flats—where people don't know their neighbours—not even their next-door ones. But in this block of flats, everybody is friends with everybody else. We are one big, happy family. I am sure that you will be very happy here.'

The well-dressed lady got a shock when she came to visit the flat the next time, because she found a quite different man and woman in it. Mr and Mrs Jones had not had the courage to tell her that they were not the *new* owners of the flat, who were due to move in the next day, but the *old* owners, who had lived beside her for two years without her ever having visited them or even noticed their existence.

16

Mr Brown was at the theatre. He had got his ticket at the last moment, so he had not been able to choose his seat. He now found that he was in the middle of a group of American ladies, some of them middle-aged and some quite old. They obviously all knew each other well, as, before the curtain went up on the play they had come to see, they all talked and joked a lot together.

The lady sitting on Mr Brown's left, who was about sixty years old, seemed to be the happiest and the most amusing of the American group, and after the first act of the play, she apologized to him for the noisiness of her friends. He answered that he was very glad to see American ladies so obviously enjoying their visit to England, and so they got into conversation. Mr Brown's neighbour explained what they were doing there.

'You know, I have known these ladies all my life,' she said. 'We all grew up together back in our home town in the United States. They have all lost their husbands, and call themselves the Merry Widows. It is a sort of club, you know. They go abroad every summer for a month or two and have a lot of fun. They always go everywhere together. I have wanted to join their club for a long time, but I didn't qualify for membership until the spring of this year.'

17

Mr and Mrs Brown were going abroad for their holiday. They had a dog called Blackie which they were very fond of, but they could not take him abroad with them, so they looked for a good place to leave him while they were away, and at last found a place which looked after dogs very well while their owners were away. They took Blackie there just before they left for their holiday, and sadly said goodbye to him.

At the end of their holiday, they got back to England very late at night, and as they thought that the place where Blackie was staying might be closed at that late hour, they decided to wait until the next morning before going to get him.

So the next morning Mr Brown got into his car and drove off happily to collect Blackie.

When he reached home with the dog, he said to his wife, 'Do you know, dear, I don't think Blackie can have enjoyed his stay at that place very much. He barked all the way home in the car as if he wanted to tell me something.'

Mrs Brown looked at the dog carefully and then answered, 'You are quite right, dear. He was certainly trying to tell you something. But he wasn't trying to tell you that he hadn't enjoyed his stay at that place. He was only trying to tell you that you were bringing the wrong dog home. This isn't Blackie!'

18

Nasreddin sat drinking coffee and talking with some of his old friends. One of the things they discussed was the difference between one person's sense of values and another's. After some minutes, one of Nasreddin's friends said to him, 'Well, Nasreddin, you are a wise man, but you have said nothing on this subject yet. What do *you* consider to be the most valuable thing in the world?'

Nasreddin answered without hesitation, 'I consider advice the most valuable thing in the world.'

His friends thought about this for a few moments, and then one of them asked him, 'And what do you consider the most worthless thing in the world?'

Again Nasreddin replied without hesitating for a moment, 'I consider advice the most worthless thing in the world.'

'Really!' said one of his friends. 'You must be joking, Nasreddin! A minute ago you said that advice is the most *valuable* thing in the world, and now you say that it is the most *worthless* thing in the world! How can it be both the most valuable and the most worthless?'

'Well,' answered Nasreddin, 'if you think about the matter carefully, you will see that I am not joking, and that I am quite right. When you give somebody good advice, and he takes it, advice is the most valuable thing in the world. But when you give a person advice and he does not take it, it is the most worthless thing in the world.'

19

Mrs Jones was over eighty, but she still drove her old car like a woman half her age. She loved driving very fast, and boasted of the fact that she had never, in her thirty-five years of driving, been punished for a driving offence.

Then one day she nearly lost her record. A police car followed her, and the policemen in it saw her pass a red light without stopping.

When Mrs Jones came before the judge, he looked at her severely and said that she was too old to drive a car, and that the reason why she had not stopped at the red light was most probably that her eyes had become weak with old age, so that she had simply not seen it.

When the judge had finished what he was saying, Mrs Jones opened the big handbag she was carrying and took out her sewing. Without saying a word, she chose a needle with a very small eye, and threaded it at her first attempt.

When she had successfully done this, she took the thread out of the needle again and handed both the needle and the thread to the judge, saying, 'Now it is your turn. I suppose *you* drive a car, and that you have no doubts about your own eyesight.'

The judge took the needle and tried to thread it. After half a dozen attempts, he had still not succeeded. The case against Mrs Jones was dismissed, and her record remained unbroken.

20

When a big ship is in very rough sea, it has to be able to bend a little, otherwise it may break in two. If one end of the ship is on the top of one huge wave, and the other end is on the top of another, with the middle of the ship hanging in between; or if one huge wave comes up under the middle of the ship, leaving the two ends hanging, the ship's own weight will break its back if it is quite stiff.

To make a big ship elastic enough to avoid this danger, it has joints where the sections of the ship come together above the water-line, and these joints open and shut slightly as the waves lift one section of the ship or another. This is enough to save the ship from breaking into pieces.

One day a sailor was walking along a passage-way in a big ship during a storm when he was surprised to see a boy sitting comfortably in a chair at the end of the passage-way, which was opposite one of the ship's joints. The boy had a bag of nuts beside him, and every time the ship was lifted by a wave and the joint opened, he put a nut in it. As the ship came down again, the joint closed and cracked the nut, gently but firmly. The boy then took it out and put the next one in as the joint opened again.

21

Dick was a clever boy, but his parents were poor, so he had to work in his spare time and during his holidays to pay for his education. In spite of this, he managed to get to the university, but it was so expensive to study there that during the holidays he found it necessary to get two jobs at the same time so as to earn enough money to pay for his studies.

One summer he managed to get a job in a butcher's shop during the daytime, and another in a hospital at night. In the shop, he learnt to cut meat up quite nicely, so the butcher often left him to do all the serving while he went into a room behind the shop to do the accounts. In the hospital, on the other hand, he was, of course, allowed to do only the simplest jobs, like helping to lift people and to carry them from one part of the hospital to another. Both at the butcher's shop and at the hospital, Dick had to wear white clothes.

One evening at the hospital, Dick had to help to carry a woman from her bed to the place where she was to have an operation. The woman was already feeling frightened at the thought of the operation before he came to get her, but when she saw Dick, that finished her.

'No! No!' she cried. 'Not my butcher! I won't be operated on by my butcher!' and fainted away.

22

Nasreddin was a poor man, so he tried to grow as many vegetables as he could in his own garden, so that he would not have to buy so many in the market.

One evening he heard a noise in his garden and looked out of the window. A white ox had got into the garden and was eating his vegetables. Nasreddin at once took his stick, ran out and chased the ox, but he was too old to catch it. When he got back to his garden, he found that the ox had ruined most of his precious vegetables.

The next morning, while he was walking in the street near his house, he saw a cart with two white oxen which looked very much like the one that had eaten his vegetables. He was carrying his stick with him, so he at once began to beat the two oxen with it. As neither of them looked more like the ox that had eaten his vegetables than the other, he beat both of them equally hard.

The owner of the ox-cart was drinking coffee in a nearby coffee-house. When he saw what Nasreddin was doing to his animals, he ran out and shouted, 'What are you doing? What have those poor animals done to you for you to beat them like that?'

'You keep out of this!' Nasreddin shouted back. 'This is a matter between me and one of these two oxen. *He* knows very well why I am beating him!'

23

The war had begun, and George had joined the air force. He wanted to be a pilot, and after some months he managed to get to the air force training school, where they taught pilots to fly.

There, the first thing that new students had to do was to be taken up in a plane by an experienced pilot, to give them some idea of what it felt like. Even those who had travelled as passengers in commercial airline planes before found it strange to be in the cockpit of a small fighter plane, and most of the new students felt nervous.

The officer who had to take the students up for their first flight allowed them to fly the plane for a few seconds if they wanted to and if they were not too frightened to try, but he was always ready to take over as soon as the plane started to do dangerous things.

George was one of those who took over the controls of the plane when he went up in it for the first time, and after the officer had taken them from him again, George thought that he had better ask a few questions to show how interested he was and how much he wanted to learn to fly. There were a number of instruments in front of him, so he chose one and asked the officer what it was.

The officer looked at him strangely for a moment and then answered, 'That—is the clock.'

24

Mr Robinson had to travel somewhere on business, and as he was in a hurry, he decided to go by air. He liked sitting beside a window when he was flying, so when he got on to the plane, he looked for a window seat. He found that all of them had already been taken except for one. There was a soldier sitting in the seat beside this one, and Mr Robinson was surprised that he had not taken the one by the window; but, anyhow, he at once went towards it.

When he reached it, however, he saw that there was a notice on it. It was written in ink and said, 'This seat is reserved for proper load balance. Thank you.' Mr Robinson had never seen such a notice in a plane before, but he thought that the plane must be carrying something particularly heavy in its baggage room which made it necessary to have the passengers properly balanced, so he walked on and found another empty seat, not beside a window, to sit in.

Two or three other people tried to sit in the window seat beside the soldier, but they too read the notice and went on. Then, when the plane was nearly full, a very beautiful girl stepped into the plane. The soldier, who was watching the passengers coming in, quickly took the notice off the seat beside him—and in this way succeeded in having the company of the girl during the whole of the trip.

25

Mrs Jones was very fond of singing. She had a good voice, except that some of her high notes tended to sound like a gate which someone had forgotten to oil. Mrs Jones was very conscious of this weakness, and took every opportunity she could find to practise these high notes. As she lived in a small house, where she could not practise without disturbing the rest of the family, she usually went for long walks along the country roads whenever she had time, and practised her high notes there. Whenever she heard a car or a person coming along the road, she stopped and waited until she could no longer be heard before she started practising again, because she was a shy person, and because she was sensitive about those high notes.

One afternoon, however, a fast, open car came up behind her so silently and so fast that she did not hear it until it was only a few metres from her. She was singing some of her highest and most difficult notes at the time, and as the car passed her, she saw an anxious expression suddenly come over its driver's face. He put his brakes on violently, and as soon as the car stopped, jumped out and began to examine all his tyres carefully.

Mrs Jones did not dare to tell him what the noise he had heard had really been, so he got back into his car and drove off as puzzled as he had been when he stopped.

26

April 1st is a day on which, in some countries, people try to play tricks on others. If one succeeds in tricking somebody, one laughs and says, 'April Fool!', and then the person who has been tricked usually laughs too.

One April 1st, a country bus was going along a winding road when it slowed down and stopped. The driver anxiously turned switches and pressed buttons, but nothing happened. Then he turned to the passengers with a worried look on his face and said, 'This poor bus is getting old. It isn't going as well as it used to. There's only one thing to do if we want to get home today. I shall count three, and on the word 'three', I want you all to lean forward suddenly as hard as you can. That should get the bus started again, but if it doesn't, I am afraid there is nothing else I can do. Now, all of you lean back as far as you can in your seats and get ready.'

The passengers all obediently pressed back against their seats and waited anxiously.

Then the driver turned to his front and asked, 'Are you ready?'

The passengers hardly had enough breath to answer, 'Yes.'

'One! Two! *Three*!' counted the driver. The passengers all swung forward suddenly—and the bus started up at a great rate.

The passengers breathed more easily and began to smile with relief. But their smiles turned to surprised and then delighted laughter when the driver merrily cried, 'April Fool!'

27

The women's college had a very small car-park, and as several of the teachers and students, and many of the students' boy-friends, had cars, it was often difficult to find a place to park. The head of the college, whose name was Miss Baker, therefore had a special place in the car-park for her own small car. There were white lines round it, and it had a notice saying, 'Reserved for Head of College'.

One evening, however, when Miss Baker got back to the College a few minutes before the time by which all students had to be in, she found another car in her parking space. There were two people in it, one of her girl-students and a young man. Miss Baker knew that the young man would have to leave very soon, so she decided to ask him to move his car a bit, so that she could park hers in the proper place for the night before going to bed.

As the young man's car was close to the railings, Miss Baker had to drive up beside it on the other side, where the girl was sitting. She therefore came up on this side, opened her own window and tapped her horn lightly to draw attention to the fact that she was there. The girl, who had her head on the boy's shoulder, looked around in surprise. She was even more surprised when she heard Miss Baker say, 'Excuse me, but may I change places with you?'

28

The soldiers had just arrived in France. None of them could speak any French, except Harry, who boasted that he knew the language very well. The other soldiers did not really believe him, because they knew that he was always boasting about something, and that what he said about himself was seldom true.

For some days, the soldiers were all kept in camp, so they had no need or opportunity to speak any French. But then the day came when they were allowed to leave for the weekend.

'Now we can see whether you really speak French or not,' they said to Harry.

'All right,' Harry answered. 'Come with me, and I will show you.'

About ten minutes after they had left the camp, they saw a pretty girl of about twenty on the other side of the road. They would all have liked to speak to her, but of course none of them knew any French except (perhaps) Harry.

'Now is your chance to show us whether you can really speak French, Harry,' said one of his friends. 'Go and speak to that girl.'

'All right,' Harry answered, and he crossed the road, smiled, bowed politely to the girl and started to speak to her. He had said only a few sentences when the girl's face turned red and she smacked his face angrily and walked off.

Harry crossed the road to his friends again, his face all smiles, and said, 'There you are! I told you I could speak French, didn't I?'

29

When sailors are allowed ashore after a long time at sea, they sometimes get drunk and cause trouble. For this reason, the navy always has naval police in big ports. When sailors cause trouble, the naval police come and deal with them.

One day, the naval police in one big seaport received an urgent telephone call from a bar in the town. The barman said that a big sailor had got drunk and was breaking the furniture in the bar. The petty officer[1] who was in charge of the naval police guard that evening said that he would come immediately.

Now, petty officers who had to go and deal with sailors who were violently drunk usually chose the biggest naval policeman they could find to go with them. But this particular petty officer did not do this. Instead, he chose the smallest and weakest-looking man he could find to go to the bar with him and arrest the sailor who was breaking the furniture.

[1] 'Petty officer' is a rank in the Navy. It is above a sailor, but below a full officer.

Another petty officer who happened to be there was surprised when he saw the petty officer of the guard choose this small man, so he said to him, 'Why don't you take a big man with you? You may have to fight the sailor who is drunk.'

'Yes, you are quite right,' answered the petty officer of the guard. 'That is exactly why I am taking this small man. If you saw two policemen coming to arrest you, and one of them was much smaller than the other, which one would *you* attack?'

30

The manager of a small building company was very surprised to get a bill for two white mice which one of his workmen had bought. He sent for the workman and asked him why he had had the bill sent to the company.

'Well,' the workman answered, 'you remember the house we were repairing in Newbridge last week, don't you? One of the things we had to do there was to put in some new electric wiring. Well, in one place we had to pass some wires through a pipe thirty feet long and about an inch across, which was built into solid stone and had four big bends in it. None of us could think how to do this until I had a good idea. I went to a shop and bought two white mice, one of them male and the other female. Then I tied a thread to the body of the male mouse and put him into the pipe at one end, while Bill held the female mouse at the other end and pressed her gently to make her squeak. When the male mouse heard the female mouse's squeaks, he rushed along the pipe to help her. I suppose he was a gentleman even though he was only a mouse. Anyway, as he ran through the pipe, he pulled the thread behind him. It was then quite easy for us to tie one end of the thread to the electric wires and pull them through the pipe.'

The manager paid the bill for the white mice.

31

Nasreddin was friendly with most of his neighbours, but there was one woman who lived in his street whom he had always disliked. She was too interested in other people's business, and too ready to talk about it with others. And she was always borrowing things from her neighbours and then forgetting to return them.

This woman knew that Nasreddin had a new rope in his shed, and one day she came to his door and asked to borrow it.

'Well,' said Nasreddin, 'before I lend you my rope, I must know what you want it for.'

'One of our neighbours is cutting a big branch off the tree in my garden,' she answered, 'and he needs the rope to pull it down with, so that it does not fall on my roof.'

'Hasn't he got a rope himself?' asked Nasreddin.

'No, he hasn't,' the woman answered rudely. 'Do you think I would have come here to get yours if he had had one?'

Nasreddin said nothing, but went into his house. The woman heard him talking to his wife, and a moment later he came out again. 'I am sorry,' he said to the woman, 'but I cannot lend you the rope just now. My wife is spreading flour on it.'

'Spreading flour on it?' the woman cried. 'But how can anyone spread flour on a rope? Are you trying to make a fool out of me?'

'Certainly not!' answered Nasreddin. 'It is quite easy to spread flour on my rope when I do not wish to lend it to somebody.'

32

It was Saturday, so Mr Smith did not have to go to work. It had snowed heavily the night before, and Mr Smith's young son Bobby had a new sledge, which he was very eager to try out. There was a good slope in a park not far from the Smiths' house, which children often used for their sledges, so Mr Smith agreed to take Bobby there in the car. They put the sledge in and went off.

When they reached the park, they found that there were already a lot of boys there with their sledges. They were sliding down the slope at great speed, and then pulling their sledges up again for another go.

After a few minutes Mr Smith noticed that there was one poorly-dressed little boy there who did not have a sledge. This boy had flattened out an old cardboard box, and was sliding down the slope on that. Mr Smith felt very sorry for this poor boy, and determined to ask Bobby to lend him his sledge a few times.

But before he could catch Bobby to speak to him, he was surprised—and delighted—to notice that several of the older boys in the park were lending the poor boy their sledges. Mr Smith watched them carefully—and suddenly realized that the bigger boys were not doing this because they felt sorry for the poor boy, but because they enjoyed riding on his cardboard box more than on their expensive sledges. They were actually waiting impatiently for a turn on the flattened cardboard box!

33

Jack was young, rich, and fond of girls. He hardly ever did any work, and spent most of his time enjoying himself.

One summer he bought a big motor-boat. As soon as it was ready to go to sea, he telephoned to one of the girls he had met somewhere, and invited her for a trip in his new motor-boat. It was the first of many successful invitations of this kind.

The way Jack used to invite a girl for a trip in his boat was like this: he would begin by saying, 'Hullo, Laura (or whatever the girl's name was). I have just bought a beautiful new motor-boat, and I would like to take you out for a trip in it.'

The girl's answer was usually cautious, because everybody in that part of the country knew Jack's reputation with girls. She would say something like this: 'Oh, really? That's nice. What name have you given to the boat?'

Jack would then answer, 'Well, Laura, I have named it after you.'

Of course, the girl would feel very proud that Jack had chosen *her* name for the boat out of the names of all his many girl-friends, and she would think that Jack must really love her. She would therefore be quite willing to accept his invitation to go for a trip in his motor-boat.

It would not be until she got down to the harbour and actually saw the boat that she would understand how cleverly Jack had tricked her. Because there in neat gold letters on the boat she would see its name—'After You'.

34

Night had come. There had been a big battle that day, and our army had taken the enemy's front line and then advanced half a mile beyond it. We were now in a trench which the enemy had dug as a last line of defence, and we could hear them digging themselves a new trench from which to face us in the morning. They dug in the stony soil all night, and by the morning we could see only the tops of their caps and their spades as they threw the earth out.

In our trench, several of our soldiers spent the time after daylight had come shooting at the enemy caps and spades to see if they could hit any of them.

One of the enemy soldiers, who seemed to be a sportsman, joined in our game. He would suddenly put his spade up, keep it there for a few seconds to see whether one of us could hit it, and then pull it down quickly again. Next time he would put it up in rather a different place. A number of our soldiers shot at it whenever it came up, but none of them seemed to succeed in hitting it.

Then there came a time when the spade remained down for much longer than usual. We thought that the soldier might have been stopped from playing this game by an officer, or that he might have gone off for a meal or something. But just when we thought that we would not see his spade again, it came up once more, for the last time—very slowly, and with a bandage tied around it.

35

George and his friend Peter were fond of deer-hunting, and whenever they had a free day during the deer-hunting season, they took their guns and went off into the forest.

One Saturday they were sitting on a log eating their sandwiches and drinking their coffee when they saw a man walking through the snow towards them. He was dressed in deer-hunting clothes, but he had no gun with him. When he got nearer, the two friends saw that he was following a deer's track in the snow. They were both very surprised to see a man tracking a deer without a gun, so when he reached them, they stopped him and asked him whether anything was wrong and whether they could help him. The man sat down beside them, accepted a cup of coffee and told them his story.

Like them, he had gone out deer-hunting that morning with a friend. They had seen a deer with very big horns, and had followed it for some time. Then he had fired at it, and it had fallen just where it stood. He and his friend had run over to examine it, and he had said to his friend, 'This deer's horns will make a wonderful rack for my guns when I get it home.' He had then arranged his gun in the deer's horns and stepped back a few yards to see exactly how they would look as a gun rack on the wall of his study. He had been admiring the effect when the deer had suddenly jumped up, shaken itself and raced away, carrying his gun firmly stuck in its horns.

36

In many seaside towns there are telescopes on the sea-front so that people who want to look at the view or at ships on the sea can do so more easily. You have to put a coin in before you can use the telescope, and after a few minutes you have to put in another coin if you want to continue using it.

One day Mr Brown was on holiday in a seaside town which had telescopes like this, and he was walking along the sea-front when he saw two sailors looking through one. First one was looking, and then the other, and they were taking turns to put in another coin from time to time.

Mr Brown was rather surprised to see sailors using the telescope, because he thought that they would have had enough of looking at the sea while they were on their ship. Then he thought that they might perhaps be looking for their own ship on the sea, but that seemed improbable to him. How could sailors not know where their ship was?

Then Mr Brown suddenly realized that they were not looking at the sea at all. The telescope was pointed at the beach, and they were looking along it slowly and carefully. Mr Brown wondered whether they had lost something.

Suddenly the sailors left the telescope and went off at a fast rate, so Mr Brown stopped wondering and continued his walk.

It was not until half an hour later that he found out what the two sailors had been searching for with the telescope. He met them again, each with a very pretty girl on his arm.

37

Mary was very fond of television, so when she met a young man who worked for a television company, she was very interested and asked him a lot of questions. She discovered that he had also worked for a film company, so she asked him whether there was any difference between film work and television work.

'Well,' answered the young man, 'there is one *very* big difference. If someone makes a mistake while a film is being made, it is, of course, possible to stop and do the scene again. In fact, one can do it over and over again a lot of times. Mistakes waste time, money and film, but the audiences who see the film when it is finished don't know that anything went wrong. In a live television show, on the other hand, the audience can see any mistakes that are made.

'I can tell you a story about that. One day, a live television show was going on, and one of the actors was supposed to have been shot. He fell to the ground, and the camera moved somewhere else to allow time for me to run out with a bottle of tomato sauce to pour on to him to look like blood. But unfortunately the camera turned back to him before I had finished, and the audience saw me pouring the sauce on to the man.'

'Oh, how terrible!' Mary said. 'And what did you do?'

'Well,' answered the young man, 'our television director is a very strict man. If anyone makes a mistake, he dismisses him at once. So what could I do? I just had to pretend that this was part of the story, and eat the man.'

38

Johnny was four years old, and his favourite game was cowboys and Indians. He had a cowboy suit and a belt with two guns, and spent most of his time pretending to be fighting Indians.

One day his mother took him in a train for the first time. Of course, he wore his cowboy suit and carried his two guns. He had seen a film of an attack by Red Indians on a train in the Wild West, so his mother was not surprised when he began playing at cowboys and Indians in the train. But when he wanted to open the window wide so that he could shoot out of it, she thought this too dangerous, and allowed him to have it open only at the top, so that he could shoot out of it if he stood up, but could not fall out.

He was playing happily, hiding behind the curtain, suddenly stepping forward, firing a shot out of the window and then quickly stepping back again, when he suddenly gave a cry, fell back on to the seat, and lay there with his chin resting on his chest and his arms hanging loosely beside him. Of course, his mother was frightened. She thought that something from outside the train must have hit him as he stood at the window. She shook the child gently, but he made no movement, and his eyes rolled in his head.

His mother was now very worried indeed. She picked Johnny up in her arms to go and find help; but just then he lifted one of his arms with great effort, pointed to his chest and said in a weak whisper, 'Pull the arrow out, will you?'

39

The science teacher believed very strongly in practical work as a means of teaching science effectively, and she wanted her pupils' parents to see how well their children were learning by her methods. She therefore arranged for all the parents to come and see the results of one of the children's experiments on a Saturday evening, when all of them were free.

The children had been studying the growth of plants, and they had planted four pots of beans a few weeks before. They had put poor soil in one pot, to see what effect this would have on the growth of the beans in it, and good soil in the other three pots. Then they had put one of the pots in the dark for several days, and had given a third pot no water for the same length of time.

At the end of the lesson on Friday afternoon, the teacher put little notices on the four pots: 'The beans in this pot were planted in poor soil.' 'This pot has been kept in the dark for four days.' 'These beans have had no water for four days.' 'These beans have had good soil, plenty of light and regular water.' Then the teacher went home.

When she arrived on Saturday evening, half an hour before the parents were due to come, she found this note beside the pots: 'We read your notes to the school servant and thought we would help him, so we watered all the plants, changed the earth in the one with poor soil, and left the light on above the one that had been left in the dark for four days. We hope that the plants will now grow better.

'Your friends,
'The Boy Scouts.'

40

King Frederick the Great of Prussia had a very fine army, and none of the soldiers in it were finer than his Giant Guards, who were all extremely tall men. It was difficult to find enough soldiers for these Guards, as there were not many men who were tall enough.

Frederick had made it a rule that no soldiers who did not speak German could be admitted to the Giant Guards, and this made the work of the officers who had to find men for them even more difficult. When they had to choose between accepting or refusing a really tall man who knew no German, the officers used to accept him, and then teach him enough German to be able to answer if the King questioned him.

Frederick sometimes used to visit the men who were on guard around his castle at night to see that they were doing their job properly, and it was his habit to ask each new one that he saw three questions: 'How old are you?' 'How long have you been in my army?' and 'Are you satisfied with your food and your conditions?' The officers of the Giant Guards therefore used to teach new soldiers who did not know German the answers to these three questions.

One day, however, the King asked a new soldier the questions in a different order. He began with, 'How long have you been in my army?' The young soldier immediately answered, 'Twenty-two years, Your Majesty.' Frederick was very surprised. 'How old are you then?' he asked the soldier. 'Six months, Your Majesty,' came the answer. At this Frederick became angry. 'Am I a fool, or are you one?' he asked. 'Both, Your Majesty,' the soldier answered politely.

41

At the time when Bill and Rose married, neither of them had much money, so they were unable to buy a house or flat. For the first few years of their married life, they therefore lived in rented flats. Then Bill's father died and left him some money, so they bought a house. When they moved into it for the first time, one of Bill's best friends sent him a bottle of wine as a present to celebrate his entry into the first house he had owned.

Bill and Rose had a lot of work to do getting their things unpacked, arranging the furniture, getting curtains and all the rest, so they forgot about the bottle of wine. In fact, they put it away in a cupboard without even unpacking it.

Bill and Rose already had two children when they moved into their new house, and a few months later, the third was born. When Rose came home from the hospital with the baby, Bill invited some friends round to celebrate its arrival, and they had a wonderful party, with plenty to eat and to drink.

After the party had been going on for some time, however, Bill found that the wine was finished. Luckily, he remembered the bottle which his friend had given him when they had moved into the new house and which was still lying unpacked in a cupboard somewhere in the house. He found it with some difficulty and brought it into the living-room where his guests were sitting. When he had unwrapped the bottle, he saw a card tied to it, so he took it and read it aloud to the others. It said, 'Bill, take good care of this one—it is the first one that is really yours!'

42

Mr Jones woke early one morning, before the sun had risen. It was a beautiful morning, so he went to the window and looked out. He was surprised to see a neatly dressed, middle-aged professor, who worked in the university just up the road from Mr Jones's house, coming from the direction of the town. He had grey hair and thick glasses, and was carrying an umbrella, a morning newspaper and a bag. Mr Jones thought that he must have arrived by the night train and decided to walk to the university instead of taking a taxi.

Mr Jones had a big tree in his garden, and the children had tied a long rope to one of its branches, so that they could swing on it.

Mr Jones was surprised to see the professor stop when he saw the rope, and look carefully up and down the road. When he saw that there was nobody in sight, he stepped into the garden (there was no fence), put his umbrella, newspaper, bag and hat neatly on the grass and took hold of the rope. He pulled it hard to see whether it was strong enough to take his weight, then ran as fast as he could and swung into the air on the end of the rope, his grey hair blowing all around his face. Backwards and forwards he swung, occasionally taking a few more running steps on the grass when the rope began to swing too slowly for him.

At last the professor stopped, straightened his tie, combed his hair carefully, put on his hat, picked up his umbrella, newspaper and bag, and continued on his way to the university, looking as quiet and correct and respectable as one would expect a professor to be.

43

An American warship once paid a visit to a port in a hot country where the British navy had a base, and the captain of the British base invited the officers of the American warship to a party ashore.

Now, Americans like their drinks to have plenty of ice in them, even in a cold climate, but at the time of the warship's visit to the British base, it was generally known that the British hardly ever had ice, even in the hottest countries. The captain of the American ship did not want to have to drink warm drinks at the British party, but it would have been very impolite to refuse the British captain's invitation, so the American captain accepted, but, an hour before the party was due to begin, sent a small boat ashore to his host with several large tins of ice from the warship's refrigerators.

When the American officers went ashore for the party, they were looking forward to having plenty of ice in their drinks. They were therefore very surprised when, on their arrival, they were served drinks with no ice in them at all. They thought that the servants might perhaps not yet have had time to unpack the ice that had been sent from the ship, but the party continued, and still there was no ice. Of course, the American officers were too polite to ask what had happened to the ice that they had sent.

When the party at last came to an end, the American captain thanked his British host for the pleasant party. Then the secret of the ice came out. The British captain thanked the American captain for it and said, 'It allowed me to have the first really cold bath I have had in this place.'

44

The soldiers had just moved to the desert, and as they had never been in such a place before, they had a lot to learn.

As there were no trees or buildings in the desert, it was, of course, very hard to hide their trucks from enemy planes. The soldiers were therefore given training in camouflage, which means ways of covering something so that the enemy cannot see where it is. They were shown how to paint their trucks in irregular patterns with pale green, yellow, and brown paints, and then to cover them with nets to which they had tied small pieces of cloth.

The driver who had the biggest truck went to a lot of trouble to camouflage it. He spent several hours painting it, preparing a net and searching for some heavy rocks with which to hold the net down. When it was all finished, he looked proudly at his work and then went off to have his lunch.

But when he came back to the truck after he had had his meal, he was surprised and worried to see that his camouflage work was completely spoilt by the truck's shadow, which was growing longer and longer as the afternoon advanced. He stood looking at it, not knowing what to do about it.

Soon an officer arrived, and he too saw the shadow, of course.

'Well,' he shouted to the poor driver, 'what are you going to do about it? If an enemy plane comes over, the pilot will at once know that there is a truck there.'

'I know, sir,' answered the soldier.

'Well, don't just stand there doing nothing!' said the officer.

'What shall I do, sir?' asked the poor driver.

'Get your spade and throw some sand over the shadow, of course!' answered the officer.

45

Some boys join the navy when they are quite young, and are then given a course of training as sailors. It is a long course, both on land and at sea, and during it the boys study things like mathematics and science as well as learning to tie knots, fire guns, and do other practical things.

One of the important things they are taught is, of course, how to swim.

In the old days, many sailors were unable to swim, but nowadays it is rare to find one that cannot.

At one school for sailor boys, the swimming instructor was very good. He had never had a boy whom he had failed to teach to swim by the time the course ended. One year, however, there was one particular boy on the training course who seemed quite unable to learn to swim. The instructor tried giving him extra lessons, he tried throwing him into the pool at the deep end, and he tried holding him up with a rope tied to the end of a fishing-rod while he attempted to swim, but he had no success at all, whatever he did. In the end, as the time drew near when the course was due to end, he had to admit defeat.

One day, he called the boy aside after the swimming lesson and said to him, 'John, I have tried very hard to teach you to swim, but I have failed—for the first time in my life. Now I want to give you a piece of advice. Listen carefully.'

'Yes, sir,' answered the boy.

'Well,' the instructor went on, 'if you are ever in a ship and it sinks, just jump over the side into the sea, go right down to the bottom and run to the shore as fast as you can. That is the only way you will save your life.'

46

Mr Richards was quite good at shooting with a rifle, and he had taken part in several competitions in his small town. He had never actually won a prize, but each time he had done well, and once he had come fourth.

Then he had to go to a big city on business for a month, and as he had nothing much to do in the evenings there, he joined the local rifle club, and spent several pleasant evenings shooting there.

The rifle club had a very good first team, which used to take part in a lot of important shooting competitions. One of these took place while Mr Richards was with them, and of course he went to see it. But one of the members of the club's team suddenly fell ill just before the match, and the captain had to choose somebody else to take his place in a hurry. He had heard that Mr Richards had taken part in several competitions already, and he had seen for himself at the club that, although he was not really up to the standard of the club's first team, he was quite a good shot. He therefore invited him to take the sick man's place.

Mr Richards felt greatly honoured to be asked to shoot for such a good team, but he also felt very nervous, because he was afraid of making a fool of himself and letting down his team.

In fact, he was so nervous that he could not keep his hands from trembling while he was shooting, with the result that he did very badly in the competition. When he took his score card to his captain, he said, 'After seeing my score, I feel like going outside and shooting myself.'

The captain looked at the card for a few seconds and then said, 'Well, you had better take *two* bullets with vou if you do that.'

47

The government wanted to put up a big office building in the capital, and had to choose an engineering company to do the work. Several big companies wanted the job, because it would bring them a lot of money if they could get it, but, of course, they could not all have it, so the government had to decide which of them should be the lucky one. They therefore appointed a government official to examine the various companies' offers, decide which were the most suitable, and then advise the Minister of Works which of them to choose.

After some months, the choice was made and work was about to begin when one of the companies which had not been successful complained to the Minister. They said that the official who had been responsible for advising him on the choice of a company to do the work had accepted bribes.

The Minister at once ordered an inquiry into the whole matter, and after a month had proof that the official had indeed taken bribes. He therefore sent for him and asked for an explanation.

The official admitted that he had taken big bribes. 'But,' he said, 'I did not just take one from the company to which I recommended that you should give the work. I took a bribe from each company to favour it in my choice of the one to recommend.'

'Well, then,' said the Minister, 'how did you finally make your choice? Did you choose the one that gave you the biggest bribe?'

'Certainly not, sir!' answered the official, deeply hurt that the Minister should accuse him of such dishonesty. 'I was very careful to take exactly the same bribe from each of the companies that were trying to get the job.'

'Then how did you choose?' asked the Minister.

'As an honest government official,' answered the man, 'I chose the company that I thought would do the work best and most cheaply, of course.'

48

The class teacher thought that hobbies were very important for every child. She encouraged all her pupils to have one, and sometimes arranged for their parents to come and see the work they had done as a result.

One Friday morning the teacher told the class that those of them who had a hobby could have a holiday that afternoon to get the things they had made as parts of their hobbies ready for their parents to see the following afternoon.

So on Friday afternoon, while those of the pupils who had nothing to show did their usual lessons, the lucky ones who had made something were allowed to go home, on condition that they returned before five o'clock to bring what they were going to show, and to arrange it.

When the afternoon lessons began, the teacher was surprised to see that Tommy was not there. He was the laziest boy in the class, and the teacher found it difficult to believe that he had a hobby. However, at a quarter to five, Tommy arrived with a beautiful collection of butterflies in glass cases. After his teacher had admired them and helped him to arrange them on a table in the classroom, she was surprised to see Tommy pick them up again and begin to leave.

'What are you doing, Tommy?' she asked. 'Those things must remain here until tomorrow afternoon. That's when the parents are coming to see them.'

'I know they are coming then,' answered Tommy, 'and I will bring them back tomorrow; but my big brother doesn't want them to be out of our house at night in case they are stolen.'

'But what has it got to do with your big brother?' asked the teacher. 'Aren't the butterflies yours?'

'No,' answered Tommy. 'They belong to him.'

'But Tommy, you are supposed to show your own hobby here, not somebody else's!' said the teacher.

'I know that,' answered Tommy. 'My hobby is watching my brother collecting butterflies.'

49

Mr Hall was a rich business man and lived in a big house beside a beautiful river.

Now, this river usually froze over in winter, and one year it did this very early, so that by Christmas time it was covered with really thick ice. One could walk across it easily, and some brave people had even crossed it in motor-cars with chains on their wheels.

The sight of this ice gave Mr Hall an idea. He decided to have a big Christmas party on the ice. He would have all the furniture and carpets in his living-room carried out on to the ice, he would have pretty coloured lights hung all around, and they would have a wonderful party. So he sent out invitations to all his important friends, and on Christmas Day they all began to arrive at his house and then go down on to the ice. They were all in very good spirits and thought that it had been a wonderful idea of Mr Hall's to have a party on the ice, surrounded by the beautiful scenery of that part of the country, but at the same time with all the comforts of armchairs, carpets, servants, good food and plenty of drinks.

The party went on until late at night, and as the last guests said their merry goodbyes, Mr Hall congratulated himself on a very successful party.

He had drunk rather a lot during the day, so he did not wake up very early the next morning. In fact, it was nearly midday before he got up and looked out of the window at the scene of the previous day's party. What he saw there made him wonder whether he was still asleep and dreaming! He closed his eyes, opened them again—but there was no mistake! The ice had broken up during the night or in the early hours of the morning and had carried all his living-room furniture, carpets and coloured lights out to sea with it!

50

Mr and Mrs Davies were invited to Christmas drinks at a hotel one year. They left their car in the car-park outside and went in. Mr Davies was proud of the fact that he never got drunk, so he was careful not to drink too much, in spite of his host's attempts to press more and more on him.

During the party, Mrs Davies found that she had forgotten to bring a handkerchief, so she asked her husband to go out to the car and get her one. He did so, but on his way back to the hotel entrance, he heard a car horn blowing in the car-park. Thinking someone might be in trouble, he went over to the car from which the noise was coming. He found a small black bear sitting in the driving-seat and blowing the horn.

When Mr Davies got back to the party, he told several people about the black bear, but of course they did not believe him and thought he was drunk. When he took them out to the car-park to show them that his story was true, he found that the car with the bear in it had gone.

There were so many jokes about Mr Davies's black bear during the following days that he at last put an advertisement in the local paper: 'Will anybody who saw a black bear blowing the horn in a car outside the Central Hotel at about 7 p.m. on Christmas Day please phone . . . .'

Two days later a Mrs Richards phoned to say that she and her husband had left their pet bear Honeypot in their car outside the Central Hotel for a few minutes that evening, and that it was quite possible that he had been blowing the horn. Mrs Richards did not seem to think there was anything strange about that. 'Honeypot *likes* blowing car horns,' she said, 'and we don't mind as long as we are not actually driving the car.'

51

A famous actor often had to travel by train. Of course, a lot of his fellow-passengers used to recognize him on his journeys, and some of them tried to get into conversation with him, but he was usually feeling tired after acting until late the night before, so he did not encourage them to talk to him.

One day he had just got into the train with all his luggage when a young man came and sat down in the seat opposite him. The young man took out a book and began to read it, while the actor tried to get some sleep in his corner of the carriage.

When he opened his eyes, he found that the young man was looking at him with his mouth open, his book forgotten. The actor shut his eyes and tried to sleep again, but every time he opened them, the young man was looking at him with the same fixed look. At last he gave up the attempt to sleep, took out a newspaper, put it up in front of him and began to read.

After a few moments the young man cleared his throat and spoke. 'I beg your pardon, sir,' he said, 'but haven't I seen you somewhere before?'

The actor did not answer. He did not even put his newspaper down.

The young man said nothing more for several minutes, but then he tried again. 'I beg your pardon, sir,' he said, 'but are you going to San Francisco?'

The actor put his paper down this time, looked at the young man severely without saying a word, and then put the paper up in front of him again.

This time there was an even longer pause before the young man spoke again. Then he said, in a last attempt to start a conversation with the great man, 'I am George P. Anderson of Wilmington, Vermont.'

This time the actor put his paper down and spoke. 'So am I,' he said.

That was the end of the conversation.

52

While Nasreddin was walking home one evening, he met four of his old friends. To be polite, he invited them to come home with him to supper. He was expecting that they would equally politely refuse his invitation, but to his surprise, they quickly accepted and went home with him.

Nasreddin was a poor man, and there was never much food in his house. He knew that there would be very little for supper that night, even for his wife and himself, but he did not know how to get rid of his unwanted guests without being very rude, so he let them come with him as far as his house. But when they were a short distance from his front door, he suddenly rushed forward, opened it, went in, shut it again and then locked it. He found his wife in the kitchen and quickly told her what had happened.

Nasreddin's guests were at first surprised at his unexpected behaviour. Then they thought that he had perhaps gone ahead to make preparations to welcome them into his house. And then, when nothing had yet happened after several minutes, they began to get angry and to bang on the door, calling at the same time for Nasreddin.

After this had gone on for some time, Nasreddin sent his wife to a window to talk to the old men. She told them that Nasreddin was not at home.

'What do you mean, he is not at home, woman?' shouted one of the men. 'We came here a few minutes ago *with* Nasreddin, and we saw him go into the house!'

Nasreddin was now afraid that the noise the old men were making would bring all his neighbours around and that he would be publicly shamed, so he put his head out of the window and said, 'Please, gentlemen, what are you making all this noise about? This house has a back door as well as a front one. Perhaps Nasreddin came in through one and went out through the other.'

53

One day, Nasreddin was walking quietly along the road when somebody gave him a violent blow on the back of the neck. He looked behind him, and saw a young man whom he had never seen before.

'How dare you hit me like that!' shouted Nasreddin.

The young man said he had mistaken Nasreddin for a friend of his and that he thought Nasreddin was making a lot of noise about nothing.

This insult made Nasreddin even angrier, of course, and he at once arranged for the young man to be brought before a judge. There was nothing for the young man to do but to appear before the court.

Now, the judge who heard the case was a friend of the young man's father, and, although he pretended to be quite fair, he was thinking how he could avoid punishing the young man while at the same time not appearing unjust.

Finally he said to Nasreddin, 'I understand your feelings in this matter very well. Would you be satisfied if I let you hit the young man as he hit you?'

Nasreddin said he would not be. The young man had insulted him and should be properly punished.

'Well, then,' said the judge to the young man, 'I order you to pay ten liras to Nasreddin.'

Ten liras was very little for such a crime, but the young man did not have it with him, so the judge allowed him to go and get it.

Nasreddin waited for him to return with the money. He waited an hour, he waited two hours, while the judge attended to other business.

When it was nearly time for the court to close, Nasreddin chose a moment when the judge was especially busy, came up quietly behind him and hit him hard on the back of the neck. Then he said to him, 'I am sorry, but I can't wait any longer. When the young man comes back, tell him that I have passed my right to the ten liras on to you.'

54

It was snowing heavily, and the wind was blowing the snow into great piles against the fences at the sides of the road. In some places the piles were so big that they were beginning to spread right across the road, but as long as cars could keep moving rather fast, they were still managing to get through.

There was one point, however, where there was a sharp bend in the road. There the snow had piled up on both sides, and as cars had to slow down to get round the corner safely, their drivers had to be very skilful to avoid getting stuck.

At last, of course, there was one who was not skilful enough and who let his car stop on the corner. When he tried to start it again, the wheels slipped, and the car finished up deep in the snow and blocking the road.

The next car to reach the corner was in trouble too. The driver had been trying to keep up a good speed to avoid getting stuck, and he did not notice the car blocking the road in front of him until he was almost on top of it. He put his brakes on hard, the wheels of his car locked, and it slid sideways into deep snow.

It was not the last to do this. Car after car came round the corner too fast to stop properly, and finished up in the deep snow at the side of the road. Before long, there were five cars stuck as the snow continued to fall.

At last, a neighbour saw what had happened and telephoned the local garage, which sent a truck to pull the cars out of the snow. The neighbour watched as the garage men pulled them out one by one. When they reached the car which had started all the trouble by getting stuck across the road, the neighbour said to them, 'You aren't going to move that one, are you? That's the one that has brought you all this business today!'

55

One day Nasreddin went to visit King Tamerlane, who took him to see his horses and donkeys, of which he was very proud. Nasreddin naturally wanted to please the King, so he praised each of the animals greatly.

At last they came to a beautiful cream-coloured donkey which Tamerlane had bought the week before.

'What a wonderfully clever animal it looks!' cried Nasreddin. 'I am sure it could learn to read, Your Majesty!'

As soon as he had said this, he regretted his words, but it was too late to take them back any more.

Tamerlane looked at Nasreddin. 'Well, well,' he said after a few moments, 'so you believe that you could teach my donkey to read, do you? Well, you have one month to do so.'

Nasreddin knew what the King would do to him if he did not succeed in teaching the donkey to read. He took the animal's rope and led it to his own house, feeling very unhappy indeed.

Exactly a month later, he went to see the King again with the donkey and a very big book. He put the book in front of the donkey, and the animal began to turn the pages eagerly with its tongue. When it reached the middle of the book, it stopped and began to bray loud and long.

Tamerlane roared with laughter and then said to Nasreddin, 'How did you teach it to do this trick?'

Nasreddin took a deep breath of relief and then said, 'Well, Your Majesty, I first put some hay between the first and the second pages, so that the donkey had to turn the first page with his tongue to get the hay. Then the next day, I put the hay between the second and the third pages, so that he had to turn two pages to get the hay. On the third day he had to turn three pages, and so on. Today he brayed because he was angry and disappointed when he did not find any hay in the book at all.'

56

One day some wise men, who were going about the country trying to find answers to some of the great questions of their time, came to Nasreddin's district and asked to see the wisest man in the place. Nasreddin was brought forward, and a big crowd gathered to listen.

The first wise man began by asking, 'Where is the exact centre of the world?'

'It is under my right heel,' answered Nasreddin.

'How can you prove that?' asked the first wise man.

'If you don't believe me,' answered Nasreddin, 'measure and see.'

The first wise man had nothing to answer to that, so the second wise man asked his question.

'How many stars are there in the sky?' he said.

'As many as there are hairs on my donkey,' answered Nasreddin.

'What proof have you got of that?' asked the second wise man.

'If you don't believe me,' answered Nasreddin, 'count the hairs on my donkey and you will see.'

'That is foolish talk,' said the other. 'How can one count the hairs on a donkey?'

'Well,' answered Nasreddin, 'how can one count the stars in the sky? If one is foolish talk, so is the other.' The second wise man was silent.

The third wise man was becoming annoyed with Nasreddin and his answers, so he said, 'You seem to know a lot about your donkey, so can you tell me how many hairs there are in its tail?'

'Yes,' answered Nasreddin. 'There are exactly as many hairs in its tail as there are in your beard.'

'How can you prove that?' said the other.

'I can prove it very easily,' answered Nasreddin. 'You can pull one hair out of my donkey's tail for every one I pull out of your beard. If the hairs on my donkey's tail do not come to an end at exactly the same time as the hairs in your beard, I will admit that I was wrong.'

Of course, the third wise man was not willing to do this, so the crowd declared Nasreddin the winner of the day's arguments.

57

It was a very wide river, with many great curves in it, and in one of these there lived a large number of wild pigs. Nobody could remember how they had got there, but they managed to live through floods, fires, ice and attacks by hunters.

Then one day a stranger came to the nearest village and asked where he could find the wild pigs. Somebody told him, and he went off. He had no weapons with him, and the village people wondered what he was going to do with the pigs.

When he came back a few months later and said that he had caught all the pigs, the villagers were still more surprised, but some of the men agreed to go with him when he asked for help in bringing the pigs out. They wanted to see whether he was telling the truth.

Indian Corn

They soon discovered that he was. All the pigs were inside an enclosure which had a fence round it and a gate in one of its sides.

'How did you do it?' they asked the stranger.

'Well, it was quite easy really,' he answered. 'I began by putting out some Indian corn. At first, they would not touch it, but after a few weeks, some of the younger pigs began to run out of the bushes, take some of the corn quickly, and then run back. Soon all the pigs were eating the corn I put out. Then I began to build a fence round the corn. At first it was very low, but gradually I built it higher and higher without frightening the pigs away. When I saw that they were waiting for me to bring the corn each day instead of going and searching for their own food as they had done in the past, I built a gate in my fence and shut it one day while they were all eating inside the enclosure. I can catch any animal in the world in the same way if I can get it into the habit of depending on me for its food.'

58

Although Nasreddin was a poor man, he decided one day to take King Tamerlane a roast goose as a present.

Now, Nasreddin had not had much to eat that day, and soon the smell of the roast goose as he carried it to the King became too much for him, so he tore off one of its legs and ate it.

When he came before the King and offered him the goose, Tamerlane at once noticed that one of the legs was missing. Now, he had himself been born with one bad leg, so that he had never been able to walk properly. When he saw that the goose that Nasreddin was offering him had only one leg, he therefore thought that Nasreddin had done this on purpose to remind him of his own leg. Of course, he was very angry, and as he was a man who was not slow to punish those who angered him, Nasreddin was very frightened.

'Where is the goose's other leg?' the King shouted.

'Your Majesty,' answered Nasreddin trembling, 'all the geese in this part of the country have one leg only.'

'So you think I am a fool, do you?' Tamerlane answered.

'Certainly not, Your Majesty,' said Nasreddin. 'If Your Majesty will look out of the window, you will see geese with one leg by the side of your pond.'

Tamberlane looked out of the window, and there the geese were, resting on one leg beside the water. The King at once ordered one of his servants to chase the birds away. The servant took a big stick and threw it at them, and of course, they put down their other legs and ran away.

'There,' said Tamerlane. 'You were lying, Nasreddin. That shows that the geese in this part of the country have two legs, like all other geese.'

'I beg your pardon, Your Majesty,' answered Nasreddin, 'but it doesn't show anything of the kind. If your servant threw a big stick like that at *me*, I might grow *two* more legs myself to help me to run away faster.'

59

A certain hunter had found a piece of forest where there were plenty of animals to hunt. The only trouble was that the place was very difficult to get to.

He returned from his first visit to the place in late autumn, and could not get back until the snows melted in the following spring. Then he went to the pilot of a small plane, who earned his living by carrying hunters over parts of the country where there were no roads and no railways, and asked him to take him back to his favourite piece of forest.

The pilot did not know the place, so the hunter showed it to him on the map. 'But there is nowhere to land there, man!' said the pilot. 'I have flown over that part of the country on my way to other places, and I know that we can't land anywhere between this river and these mountains.'

'I thought you were a wonderful pilot,' said the hunter. 'Some of my friends said you could land a plane on a postage stamp.'

'That's right,' answered the pilot. 'I can land a plane where nobody else can. But I tell you there is nowhere to land in the place you are talking about.'

'And what if I tell you that another pilot *did* land me there last spring?' said the hunter.

'Is that true?' asked the pilot.

'Yes, it is. I swear it.'

Well, this pilot could not let himself be beaten by another, so he agreed to take the hunter.

When they reached the place, the hunter pointed out a small spot without trees in the middle of the forest, with a steep rise at one end. The pilot thought that there was not enough room to land there, but the hunter said that the other pilot had done so the year before, so down went the plane. When it came to the rise, it turned right over onto its back. As the hunter climbed out, he smiled happily and said, 'Yes, that is exactly how the other pilot managed it last time.'

60

George had stolen some money, but the police had caught him and he had been put in prison. Now his trial was about to begin, and he felt sure that he would be found guilty and sent to prison for a long time.

Then he discovered that an old friend of his was one of the members of the jury at his trial. Of course, he did not tell anybody, but he managed to see his friend secretly one day. He said to him, 'Jim, I know that the jury will find me guilty of having stolen the money. I cannot hope to be found not guilty of taking it—that would be too much to expect. But I should be grateful to you for the rest of my life if you could persuade the other members of the jury to add a strong recommendation for mercy to their statement that they consider me guilty.'

'Well, George,' answered Jim, 'I shall certainly try to do what I can for you as an old friend, but of course I cannot promise anything. The other eleven people on the jury look terribly strong-minded to me.'

George said that he would quite understand if Jim was not able to do anything for him, and thanked him warmly for agreeing to help.

The trial went on, and at last the time came for the jury to decide whether George was guilty or not. It took them five hours, but in the end they found George guilty, with a strong recommendation for mercy.

Of course, George was very pleased, but he did not have a chance to see Jim for some time after the trial. At last, however, Jim visited him in prison, and George thanked him warmly and asked him how he had managed to persuade the other members of the jury to recommend mercy.

'Well, George,' Jim answered, 'as I thought, those eleven men were very difficult to persuade, but I managed it in the end by tiring them out. Do you know, those fools had all wanted to find you not guilty!'

A 2,075 headword vocabulary

The stories in this book are written within the limits of the 2,075-word vocabulary that appears in the following pages, with the exception of the following additional words:

boarding-house, bray, butcher, camouflage, cockpit, giant, goose (pl. geese), instructor, jury, majesty, ox (pl. oxen), petty, rack, sledge, squeak, tomato, trench.

(*a.*) means adjective [and adverb]; (*adv.*) means adverb; (*conj.*) means conjunction; (*n.*) means noun; (*v.*) means verb. Letters enclosed in this way (//) show pronunciations in international phonetic script. Parts of a word enclosed in [ ] show optional additions (e.g. 'accident[al]' shows that both 'accident' and 'accidental' are included). / is used to separate alternatives (e.g. 'air[force/line/mail/port/tight]' shows that one can have 'air', 'air force', 'airline', 'airmail', 'airport' and 'airtight'). [/ shows that what precedes must be modified before what follows is added (e.g. in 'absent[/ce]', the 't' of 'absent' has to be dropped before 'ce' is added, producing 'absence', not ⇡ 'absentce'). ⇡ warns the reader that the word that follows is not correct English.

a[n]	advance[d]	alone
[un] able	[dis] advantage	along[side]
(ability/enable)	adventure	already
about	advertise[ment]	also
above	advice/advise	[al]though
abroad	[aero]plane	altogether
absent[/ce]	affair	always
absolute	affect	a.m.
accept[ed]	afford	ambition[/ious]
accident[al]	afraid	ambulance
according	after[noon]	among[st]
account	again	amount
accurate	against	amuse[/ing/ment]
accuse[/ation/d]	age	anchor
accustom	agent[/cy]	ancient
ache	ago	and
acid	[dis] agree[ment]	anger[/ry]
across	agriculture[/al]	angle
act[ing/ion/ive/ivity/	ahead	animal
or/ress]	aim[less]	ankle
actual	air[force/line/	annoy[ance/ed/ing]
add[ition]	mail/port/	answer
address	tight]	ant
admire[/ation]	algebra	anxious[/iety]
admit[/ssion]	all	any[how]
adopt[ed]	allow[ance]	apart
adult	almost	apology[/ize]

49

[dis] appear[ance]
applaud[/se]
apple
[mis] apply[/ication/ied]
appoint[ment]
[dis] approve[/al]
arch[ed/way]
argue[/ment]
arithmetic
arm
　　([un]armed)
armour
army
arrange[ment]
arrest
arrive[/al]
arrow
art[centre/
　　ist[ic]/school]
article
artificial
as
ash[tray]
ask
association
astonish[ed/ing/ment]
at
attack
attempt
attend[ance/ant/
　　tion/tive]
attract[ion/ive]
audience
aunt
autumn
avenue
average
avoid[ance]
　　(unavoidable)
away
awkward[ness]
axe

baby
back (a.)
back[bone/ground/
　　ward]
bad[ness]
bag[gage]
bake[r]
balance
ball
balloon
banana
band[stand]
bandage
bank[er]

bar
barber
bare[headed/legged]
bargain
bark
barrel
base (n. & v.)
basin
basis
basket
bath[room/tap]
　　(bathe)
battery
battle
bay

be[ing]
beach
bead
beak
beam
bean
bear (n.)
bear (v.)
beard
beast
beat[en/ing]
beauty[/iful]
because
become
bed[clothes/ding/
　　room]
bee
beer
before
beg[gar]
begin[ning]
behave[/iour]
behind
believe[/f]
bell
belong
below
belt
bench
bend
beneath
berry
beside
besides
between
beyond
bicycle
big
bill
bind[ing]
　　(bound)
bird
birth[day[-cake]/place]

biscuit
bit
bite
bitter[ness]
black[-bearded/
　　board]
blade
blame
blanket
bless[èd/ing]
blind[ing]
block
blood/bleed
blouse
blow (n.)
blow (v.)
blue[-black]
blunt
board
boast[ful]
boat
body[guard/ily]
　　(also -body, e.g. in
　　anybody)
boil[er]
bold[ness]
bomb
bone
book[-case]
boot
border
bore
bored
boredom
boring
born
borrow
both
bottle
bottom
boundary
bounds
　　(unbounded)
bow[tie]
bow (v.)
bowl (n.)
box (n.)
boy
bracelet
brain
brake
branch
brass
brave[ry]
bread
break[age]
　　(broken)
breakfast

breath[e]
bribe[ry]
brick
bridge
bright[en]
bring
broad[en]
  (breadth)
broadcast
brother
brown
bruise
brush
bucket
build[ing]
bullet
bunch
bundle
burn[ing]
burst
bury[/ial
  [ground/place]]
bus
bush[y]
business[man]
  ([un]businesslike)
busy
but
butter[-dish]
butterfly
button[-hole]
buy[er]
by

cabbage
cage
cake
[mis] calculate[/ion]
call
calm
camera
camp
can (n.)
can (v.)
canal
candle
cap
cape
capital
captain
car
card[board]
care[ful/less]
carpet
carriage
carry
cart
case

castle
cat
catch[ing]
cause
caution[/ious]
cave
ceiling
celebrate[d/ion]
cent
centre[/al]
century
ceremony[/ial/ious]
[un] certain[ty]
chain
chair[man]
chalk
chance
change
character
charcoal
charge
charm[ing]
cheap
cheat
check
cheek
cheer[ful/ing]
cheese
chemical[/ist[ry]]
cheque
chest
chew
chicken
chief
child[-bearing/
  hood/ish/like]
chimney
chin
chocolate
choose/choice
Christmas
church
cigarette[-tin]
cinema
circle[/ular]
circus
city[/izen]
civilized[/ation]
claim
class[room]
classify[/ication]
clay
clean[ness]
clear[ness]
clerk
clever
cliff
climate

climb[er/ing]
clock[work]
close (a.)
close[d]
cloth
clothe[/ing/s]
cloud[y]
club
coal[mine]
coarse
coast[-line]
coat
cock
coffee[-pot]
coin
cold[ness]
collar
collect[ion/or]
college
colony[/ial]
colour[ed/ing]
column
comb
combine[/ation/d]
come
[dis] comfort
  ([un]comfortable)
  (comforting)
command[er]
commerce[/ial]
committee
[un] common
  (commonsense)
company[/ion[ship]]
compare[/ison]
compete[/ing/ition/
  itor]
complain[t]
complete
complicated
compose[/ition/r]
concern[ing]
condition
. confess[ion]
confident[/ce]
confidential
confuse[d/ing/ion]
congratulate[/ions]
connect[ion]
conquer[ed/ing/st]
conscience
[un] conscious[ness]
consider[ation/ing]
contain[er]
[dis] content[ed]
continue[/al/ous]
control
[in] convenient[/ce]

51

conversation[al]
cook[ed/ery/ing]
cool[ness]
copper
copy
cork[screw]
corn
corner
correct[ion]
  (incorrect)
cost
cottage
cotton[-wool]
cough
council
count (v.)
country
courage[ous]
course
court[yard]
cousin
cover[ed/ing]
cow
coward[ice/ly]
crack[ed]
crash
crawl
cream
creature
creep
crime[/inal]
critic[al/ism/ize]
crop
cross (n.)
cross[ing]
crowd[ed]
crown
cruel[ty]
crush[ing]
cry
cultivate[d/ion/or]
cup
cupboard
cure
curious[/osity]
curl[ed/y]
current
curse
curtain
curve[d]
cushion[ed]
custom
cut[ting]
cycle (v.)

daddy
damage[d]
damp

dance[-band]
danger[ous]
dare[/ing]
dark[en/ness]
date
daughter
day[light/time]
  (daily)
dead[/th]
deaf[en[ing]]
deal
dear
debt
decay
deceive[/t[ful]]
decide[d/sion/sive]
deck
declare[/ation]
decorate[/ion]
decrease
deed
deep[en]
  (depth)
deer
defeat
defend[ant/ce]
degree
delay
delicate
delight[ed/ful]
deliver[y]
demand
dentist
department
depend[ant]
  ([in]dependent
  [/ce])
descend[ant]
  (descent)
describe[/ption]
desert (n.)
deserve[/ing]
desire
desk
despair[/erate]
destroy[/uction/
  uctive]
detail[ed]
determine[/ation/d]
develop[ment]
devil
diamond
dictionary
die
differ[ent[/ce]]
difficult[y]
dig
dine[/ing-hall/room]

dinner
dip
direct[ion/or]
  (misdirect)
dirt[y]
disappoint[ed/
  ing/ment]
[in] discipline
discover[er/y]
discuss[ion]
disease[d]
disgust[ed/ing]
dish
dismiss[al]
distant[/ce]
distinguish[ed/ing]
district
disturb[ance/ed]
ditch
dive[r]
divide[/sion]
do
doctor
dog
dollar
donkey
door[way]
dot
double
doubt[ful/less]
down[hill]
dozen
Dr
drag
draw[ing]
drawer
dream[y]
dress[maker/making]
drill
drink
drive[r]
drop (n.)
drop (v.)
drown
drum[mer]
drunk
dry[ness]
duck
due
dull
dumb
during
duster
dust[y]
duty

each
eager[ness]

ear[-ring]
early[/iness]
earnest
earn[ings]
earth[ly/quake]
ease[/y]
east[ern]
Easter
eat
edge
educate[/ion[al]]
  ([un]educated)
effect
  ([in]effective)
[in] efficient[/cy]
effort
egg
either
elastic[ity]
elect[ion]
electric[al/ian/ity]
elephant
else
empire[/eror]
employ[ee/er/ment]
  (unemployed
  [/ment])
empty
enclose[/ure]
encourage[ment]
end[ing/less]
enemy
engine[er[ing]]
enjoy[able/ment]
enough
enquire/inquire[/y]
enter[/rance]
entertain[ing/ment]
entire
entrust
envelope
envy[/ious]
equal[ity]
escape
[e]special
essence[/tial]
even
evening
event
  ([un]eventful)
ever[lasting]
  (and -ever, e.g. in
  whoever)
every[day/where]
evil
exact
examine[/ation/r]
example

excellent[/ce]
except[ing/ion]
excess[ive]
exchange
excite[d/ment/ing]
excuse
exercise
exist[ence/ing]
expect[ation]
expense[/ive]
experience[d]
experiment[al]
explain/explanation
explode[/sion/sive]
explore[/ation/r]
express[ion]
extend[/sion/sive/t]
extra
extraordinary
extreme
eye[brow/lash/lid/
  sight]

face[-powder]
fact
factory
fade
fail[ure]
faint[ness]
[un] fair[ness]
faith[ful]
fall[ing]
false[hood]
fame[/ous]
familiar
family
fan
fancy[/iful]
far[-reaching/ther/
  thest]
farm[er]
fashion[able]
fast (a.)
fasten[er]
fat[ness/ten/ty]
fate[/al]
father
fault[less/y]
favour[ite]
  ([un]favourable)
fear[ful/less]
feast[ing]
feather
feed
feel[ing]
fellow[ship]
female
fence

fever[ish]
few
field
fierce
fight[er]
figure
fill
film[-star]
final
find
fine[ness]
finger
finish[ed]
fire[man/place]
firm[ness]
first
fish[erman/ing-rod]
fit[ness/ting]
fix
flag
flame[/ing]
flash[ing]
flat (n.)
flat[ten]
flavour
flesh
float
flood[ed]
floor
flour
flow
flower
fly (n.)
fly
  (flight)
fog[gy]
[un] fold
follow[er/ing]
fond[ness]
food
fool[ish[ness]]
foot[ball/hold/
  path/print/step]
for
forbid[den]
force[d]
foreign[er]
forest
forget[ful[ness]]
forgive[ness]
fork
form
[in] formal[ity]
former
forth
[mis] fortune
  ([un]fortunate)
forward[s]

53

frame[work]
free[dom]
freeze
  (frozen)
frequent (*a.*)
fresh[en/ness]
friend[ly/ship]
fright[en[ed]]
from
front
fruit
fry
full
funeral
fun[ny]
fur
furnish[ed]
  (furniture)
further/furthest
future

gain
game
gap
garage
garden[er]
gas
gate[way]
gather
gay[/iety]
general (*a.*)
general (*n.*)
generous[/osity]
gentle[ness]
gentleman
geography
geometry
get
girl
give
  (gift)
glad
glass[es/y]
glory[/ious]
glue
go
goal
goat
god[dess]
  (also *god-*, e.g.
  in godson)
gold[en/-mine]
goodbye
good[ness]
goods
govern[ment/or]
  (misgovern)

grace[ful]
gradual
grain
gram
  (also *-gram*, e.g.
  in kilogram)
grammar[/tical]
gramophone
grand
  (also *grand-*, e.g.
  in grandson)
grape
grass[y]
grateful
grave[stone]
grease[/y]
great[ness]
greed[y]
green
greet[ing]
grey
grill
grind
groan
ground
group
grow[n-up/th]
growl
guard
guess
guest
guide[-book]
  (misguided)
guilt[less/y]
gun

habit
hair[y]
half[penny]
  (halve)
hall
hammer
hand[bag/ful/shake/
  writing]
handkerchief
handle
handsome
hang
happen[ing]
[un] happy[/iness]
harbour
hard[en/ness]
hardly
harm[ful/less]
harvest[-time]
haste[n/y]
hat[-stand]
hate[ful/red]

have
hay
he
head[ing/master/
  mistress]
heal
health[y]
heap
hear[er/ing]
heart
heaven[ly]
heavy
heel
help[er/fu!/ing/less]
hen
here
hesitate[/ion]
hide
high[-class/land/way]
  (height[en])
hill[side/top/y]
hinder[/rance]
hire
history[/ian/ic[al]]
hit
hobby
hold[er]
hole
holiday
hollow
holy[/iness]
home[less/made/
  work]
[dis] honest[y]
honey
[dis] honour[able]
hook
hooray/hurrah
hope[ful/less]
horizon[tal]
horn
horse[back/man/shoe]
hospital
host[ess]
hot
  (heat[ing])
hotel
hour[-hand/ly]
house[hold[er]/
  keeper/keeping/
  wife/work]
how[ever]
huge
hullo
human[ity]
humble
hunger[/ry]
hunt[er/ing]

54

hurry
hurt
husband
hut

I
ice[cream/y]
idea
ideal
idle[ness]
if
ill[ness]
imagine[/ary/
   ation/ative]
imitate[/ion]
immediate
important[/ce]
improve[d/ment]
inch
include[/ing/sive]
increase
indeed
indoor[s]
industry[/ial]
influence[/tial]
[in]flu[enza]
[mis] inform[ation]
inject[ion]
ink[pot/y]
-in-law (e.g.
   son-in-law)
in[ner[most]/to]
inn[keeper/sign]
insect
insensible
inside
instant
instead
instrument
insult[ing]
insure[/ance]
intelligent[/ce]
intend[/tion[al]]
interest[ed/ing]
interfere[nce]
interrupt[ion]
introduce[/tion]
invent[ion/or]
invite[/ation/ing]
iron
island/isle
it

jam[-dish/jar]
jar
jaw

jealous[y]
jewel[lery]
job
join[t]
joke
journalist
journey
joy[ful]
judge[/ment]
jug
juice[/y]
jump
just (adv.)
[un] just
   ([in]justice)

keep[er]
key
kick
kill
kilo[gram]
kind (n.)
[un] kind[ness]
king[dom]
kiss
kitchen
kite
knee[l]
knife
knit
knock
knot
know[ledge]
   ([un]known)

lack[ing]
ladder
lady
lake
lamp[shade]
land[ing/lord]
language
large
last (a. & n.)
last[ing]
late[ness]
lately
laugh[able/ter]
lavatory
law[less/yer]
   ([un]lawful)
lay
lazy[/iness]
lead(/led/)
lead[er[ship]]
   (mislead)

leaf[less/y]
leak
lean
learn[èd/ing]
least
leather
leave
lecture[r]
left[hand[ed]]
leg
lend/loan
less[en]
lesson
let
letter
level
liberty
library[/ian]
lick
lid
lie (n. & v.)
lie[/ar]
lift
light[en/
   hearted/ness]
light[er/house]
[un] like
   (alike)
[dis] like
[un] likely
limit[ed]
line
lion
lip[stick]
liquid
list
listen[er]
literature[/ary]
litre
little
live[/ing[-room]]
   (life[boat/less/
   like/long/size])
   (alive)
[un] load
loaf
local
lock[ed]
lodging
log
lonely[/iness]
long
   (length)
look[ing-glass]
loose[n]
lord[ship]
lose/loss/lost
lot

55

[a] loud
love[/able/r/ing]
  (beloved)
low[-class/er/land]
loyal[ty]
luck[y]
  (unlucky)
luggage
lump
lunch
lung

machine[ry]
mad[den/man/ness]
madam
magazine
mail
main[land]
make[r]
male
man[hood/kind]
manage[ment/r]
manner[s]
manufacture[r]
many
map
marbles
march
mark
market[-place]
marry[/iage/ied]
mass
master[ful/piece/y]
mat
match[box]
match[ing]
material
mathematics
matter
may
mayor
meal
mean[ing]
means
meantime/while
measure[ment]
meat
mechanical[/ism]
medical[/ine]
meet[ing]
melt
member[ship]
memory[/ial/ize]
mend
mention
merchant
mercy[/iful/iless]
mere

merry
message[/enger]
metal
metre
  (also -metre, as
  in centimetre)
midday/night
middle[-aged/class]
mild[ness]
mile
milk[bottle/jug/y]
mill[er]
mind
mine[r]
mineral
minister[/ry]
minute[-hand]
mirror
misery[/able]
miss[ing]
Miss
mistake
mix[ed/ture]
model
moderate[/ion]
modern[ize]
modest[y]
moment[ary]
money
monkey
month[ly]
moon[light]
[im] moral[ity]
  (morals)
more[over]
morning
mosque
mosquito
most[ly]
mother[-country/hood/
  ly/-tongue]
motor[-boat/
  -car/cycle]
mount[ain[ous]]
mouse[-trap]
moustache
mouth[ful]
move[ment]
  (motion[less])
Mr[s]
much
mud[dy]
multiply[/ication]
mummy
murder[er]
music[al/ian]
must
mystery[/ious]

nail
name[less]
narrow[ness]
nasty
nation
  ([inter]national)
native
nature
  ([un]natural)
navy[/al]
near
nearly
neat[ness]
[un] necessary
  (necessity)
neck[lace]
need
needle
neglect
neighbour[hood/ing]
neither
nephew
nervous[ness]
nest
net[work]
never
new
news[paper]
next
nice
niece
night[ly/time]
no[ne]
noble[man]
  (nobility)
nod
noise[/y]
noon
nor
normal
north[ern]
nose
not
note[book/paper]
notice[able/-board]
noun
now[adays]
nuisance
number
  (numerous)
nurse[ry]
nut

oar
obey[/dient[/ce]]
object (n.)

56

obiect[ion]
observe
  [/ation/r]
occasion[al]
ocean
o'clock
of
off
offend[/ce/ed]
offer
office
officer
official
often
oh
oil[y]
old[-fashioned]
  (elder/eldest)
omit[/ssion]
once
one[-sided]
  (also -one, e.g.
  in someone)
onion
only
on[to]
open[-air/ing]
operate[/ion]
opinion
opportunity
opposite
or
orange
order[ly]
ordinary
organ
organize[/ation/d]
origin[al[ity]]
ornament[al]
other[wise]
ought
out[door[s]/er[most]/
  let/line/look/
  lying/-of-door/put/
  side/spoken/
  standing]
out[number/
  weigh]
oven
over[balance/
  charge/coat/
  come/do/feed/
  flow/grown/
  hanging/head/
  joyed/look]
owe
owing to
own[er[ship]]

pack[age/ed/ing-case]
packet
pad[ded/ding]
page
pain[ful]
paint[er/ing]
pair
pale[ness]
pan
paper
parcel
pardon
  (unpardonable)
parent
park
particular
part[ing/ly/-time]
partner
party
pass[ing]
passage[-way]
passenger
passport
past
paste
pastry
path
[im] patient[/ce]
patriotic
pattern
pause
paw
pay[ment]
  (unpaid)
peace[ful]
pearl
peck
peculiar
pen
pencil[-box]
penny[worth]
people
per
perfect[ion]
perform[ance/er]
perhaps
permanent
permit[/ssion]
person[al]
persuade[/sion]
pet
petrol
photograph[er/ic/y]
physics
piano
pick
picnic
picture

piece
pig
pile
pillow
pilot
pin
pinch
pink
pipe
pity
place
plain
plan
plant[er]
plaster
plate
play[er/ground/
  thing]
[un] pleasant
[dis] please[d/ure]
plenty[/iful]
plough
plural
p.m.
pocket[-book/watch]
poem/poet[ic/ry]
point (n.)
point[ed/er]
poison[ous]
police[man]
polish
polite[ness]
politics[/al/ian]
pond
pool
poor
  (poverty)
popular[ity]
population
port
porter
position
possess[ion/or]
[im] possible[/ility]
post (n.)
post[age[stamp]/
  al/card/man/
  master/office]
postpone
pot
potato
pound
pour
powder[-puff/y]
power[ful]
practical
practice[/ise]
praise

pray[er[book]]
preach[er]
precious
prefer[able/ence]
prejudice
   ([un]prejudiced)
prepare[/ation]
present (*n. & v.*)
present[/ce]
preserve
president
press (*n.*)
press[ure]
pretend[/ce]
pretty[/iness]
prevent[ion]
price
priest
prime minister
prince[ss]
print[ed/er/ing-
   press]
prison[er]
   (imprison)
private
prize[d]
probable[/ility]
problem
procession
produce[/r/t/
   /tion/tive]
profession[al]
professor
profit
programme
progress
promise[/ing]
prompt[ness]
pronounce
   [/nunciation]
[im] proper
property
propose[/al]
protect[ion]
proud/pride
prove/proof
provide
public
pull
pump
punctual[ity]
punish[ment]
pupil
[im] pure[/ity]
purple
purpose
push[ing]
put

puzzle[/ing]

qualify[/ication/ied]
quality
quantity
quarrel[some]
quarter[ly]
queen
question[-mark]
quick[ness]
quiet[en/ness]
quite

rabbit
race[-course/-horse]
racket
radio
rail[ing/way[-line/
   -track]]
rain[bow/coat/fall/
   s/water/y]
raise
rank
rapid[ity]
rare
rash (*n.*)
rat
rate
rather
raw[ness]
ray
razor
reach
read[er/ing-room]
ready[-made]
real[ity]
realize[/ation]
reason[able[ness]]
receive[/pt/r]
recent
recite
recognize[/tion]
recommend[ation]
record
red[den/dish/-hot]
reduce[/tion]
refer[ence]
reflect[ion]
refresh[ing/ment[s]]
refrigerator
refuse[/al]
[dis] regard
   (regarding)
   (regardless)

regret
[ir] regular[ity]
rejoice[/ing[s]]
relation
relative (*n.*)
relieve[/f]
religion[/ous]
remain[ing/s]
remark
remedy
remember
remind
rent
repair
repeat[ed]
replace
reply
report[er]
represent[ative]
republic
reputation
request
rescue
reserve
resign[ation]
resist[ance]
[dis] respect[ful]
   (respectable)
responsible[/ility]
rest (*n.*)
rest[less]
restaurant
result[ing]
retire[ment]
return
revenge
review
reward
ribbon
rice
rich[es]
rid
ride[r]
rifle (*n.*)
right[angle/
   hand[ed]]
ring (*v.*)
ring[ed]
ripe[n]
rise[/ing]
   (arise)
risk[y]
rival[ry]
river[-side]
road[side]
roar
roast
rob[ber[y]]

rock[y]
rod
roll[er/ing]
roof
room
root[ed]
rope
rose
rot[ten]
rough[ness]
round[about]
  (around)
row (n.) (/rau/)
row (n. & v.)(/rou/)
royal[ty]
rub
rubber
rubbish
rude[ness]
rug
ruin[ed]
rule[r/ing]
ruler
run[ner/ning]
rush[ing]
rust[y]

sack
sacred
sacrifice
sad[den/ness]
saddle
safe[ty]
  (save[/ing])
sail[ing-ship]
sailor
sake
salary[/ied]
salt[y]
same
sample
sand[bank/hill/s/y]
sandwich
[dis] satisfy[/action/ied]
    ([un]satisfactory)
sauce
saucer
sausage
saw[dust/mill]
say[ing]
scale
scales
scarce
scatter
scene[ry]
scent[ed]

school[master/
    mistress/time]
science[/tific/tist]
scissors
scold[ing]
score
scorn[ful]
scout
scrape
scratch
scream
screen
screw[driver]
  (unscrew)
sea[bathing/blue/
    coast/level/man/
    port/shell/side/
    voyage/wall/water/
    weed]
search[ing]
season
seat
second (n.)
second[-hand]
secret[/cy]
secretary
see
seed
seem
seize
seldom
self[conscious
    [ness]/contained/
    control/defence/
    governing/
    government/
    interest/respect/
    sacrifice]
    ([un]selfish)
    (also –self/selves,
      as in myself,
      ourselves)
sell[er]
  (sale[sman])
send
sense[/ation/ible]
    ([in]sensitive)
    (nonsense[/ical])
sentence
separate[/ion]
serious[ness]
serve[/ant/ice]
set
settle[ment/r]
several
severe
sew[ing]
shade[/y]

shadow[y]
shake
shall
shallow[ness/s]
shame[ful/less]
  (ashamed)
shape[less]
share
sharp[en/ness]
shave[/ings/
    ing-brush/
    ing-soap]
she
shed
sheep
sheet
shelf
shell[-fish]
shelter
shield
shine
ship[building/ment/
    per/ping/wreck]
shirt
shock[ed/ing]
shoe[-maker]
shoot
  (shot[gun])
shop[keeper/keeping]
[a] shore
short[en/ness]
shorts
shoulder
shout
show[y]
shower
shut
shy[ness]
sick[ness/-room]
side[ways]
  (aside)
sight[seeing]
sign[ature]
sign[-post]
signal[-box]
silent[/ce]
silk[worm/y]
silly
silver[y]
simple[/icity]
since
sincere
sing[er]
single[/ular]
sink
sir
sister
sit

59

situation
size
skill[ed/ful]
skin
skirt
sky
slave[ry]
sleep[er/iness/less/y]
  (asleep)
slice
slide[/ing]
slight
slip[pery]
slope[/ing]
slow[-moving/ness]
smack (n. & v.)
small[ness]
smell
smile
smoke[d/ing[-carriage]/
  r/y]
smooth[ness]
snake
sneeze
snow[ball/shoes/
  storm/white/y]
so[-called]
soap[y]
social/society
sock
soft[en/ness]
soil (n.)
soldier
solemn
solid
solve[/ution]
some[how/times]
son
song[-book]
soon
sore
sorrow[ful]
sorry
sort
soul
sound (n. & v.)
soup
sour
south[ern]
sow (v.)
space
spade
spare
speak[er]
  (speech)
speed
spell[ing]
spend

spill
spin[ning-wheel]
spirit
spit
spite
splash
splendid
split
spoil[t]
spoon[ful]
sport[ing/sman]
spot[less/ted]
spread
spring[time]
square
squat (v.)
staff
stage
stain
stairs[/case]
  (also -stairs, e.g.
  in upstairs)
stale
stamp[-book/
  collector]
stand
standard[ize]
star
start
state (n.)
state[ment]
station
stay
[un] steady
steal
steam[boat/
  engine/er/ship]
steel
steep
steer[ing-wheel]
stem
step[ping-stone]
stick (n.)
stick[ing-plaster/y]
stiff[en/ness]
still (adv.)
still[ness]
sting
stir[ring]
stock
stocking
stomach
stone
stop[page/per]
  (non-stop)
store[-house/
  keeper/room]
storm[y]

story[-teller/-telling]
stove
straight[en]
strange[ness/r]
strap
straw
stream
street
stretch
strict
strike
string
strip
stripe[d]
stroke
strong
  (strength[en])
struggle
student
study
stuff
stupid[ity]
subject
submarine
substance
succeed[/ess[ful]]
such
suck
sudden
suffer[er/ing[s]]
sugar[-bowl]
suggest[ion]
suit (v.)
  ([un]suitable)
suit[case]
sum
summer[time]
sun[burn[t]/light/
  ny/rise/set/shine]
supper
supply
support
suppose
sure
surface
surprise[d/ing]
surround[ing[s]]
suspect[ed/icion/
  icious]
swallow (v.)
swear
sweat
sweep
sweet[en/ness]
swell[ing]
  (swollen)
swim[mer/ming-bath]
swing[ing]

60

switch
sword
sympathy[/etic[ally]/
    ize]
system

table[spoon]
tablet
tail
tailor
take
talk
tall
tame
tank
tap (*n.*)
tap (*n. & v.*)
taste[less]
tax[-collector]
taxi
tea[cup/pot/spoon]
teach[er/ings]
team
tear (/tiə/)
tear (/teə/)
telegram[/ph]
telephone
telescope
television
tell
temper
temperature
temple
tempt[ation/er/ing]
tend[ency]
tender[ness]
tennis
tent
term
terrible
test
than
thank[ful/s]
that/those
that (*conj. & rel.*)
the
theatre[/ical]
then
there
therefore
thermometer
they
thick[en/ness]
thief
thin[ness]
thing
    (also -*thing*, e.g.
    in nothing)

think[er]
thirst[y]
this/these
thorn[y]
thorough
thought[ful[ness]]
thread
threat[en[ing]]
throat
through
throw
thumb
thunder
thus
ticket
tide[/al]
tidy
tie (*n. & v.*)
tiger
tight[en]
till (*prep.*)
time[table]
tin[ned]
tip
tire[d/ing]
title
to
tobacco
today
toe
together
tomorrow
tonne
tongue
tonight
too
tool
tooth[paste]
top
torch
total
touch
tough
tour[ist]
towards
towel
tower
town[-hall]
toy
track
trade[mark/r/
    sman/-union]
traffic
train (*n.*)
train[ed/ing/
    ing-college]
translate[/ion/or]
transparent

trap[ped/ping]
travel[ler]
tray
treasure[r/y]
treat[ment]
tree
tremble
tribe
trick
trip
trouble[d/some]
trouser leg/pocket
truck
true[/th[ful[ness]]]
trumpet
trunk
trust[ed]
    (distrust)
try[/ial]
tube
tune
tunnel
turn[ing]
twice
twist
type[/ist/writer]
tyre

ugly[/iness]
umbrella
uncle
under[clothing/feed/
    ground/line/neath/
    sell/sized]
[mis] understand[ing]
union
unit
unite[/y]
universe[/al]
university
unless
until
up[-and-down/hill/
    on/per[most]/right/
    set/side-down/
    -to-date]
urge[nt]
use[d/ful[ness]/
    less[ness]/r]
used to
[un] usual

vain
valley
value[/able/less]
van

61

vary[/ious/jety]
vase
vegetable
veil[ed]
verb
verse
vertical
very
vessel
victory[/ious]
view
village[r]
violent[/ce]
violin
virtue
visit[ing-card/or]
voice
volcano
volley-ball
vote[r]
voyage

wage[s]
waist[coat]
[a] wait
waiter[/ress]
[a] wake
  (awaken)
walk[-ing-stick]
wall
wander
want
war[ship]
-ward[s] (e.g. in
  backward[s])
warm[th]
warn[ing]
wash[basin/house/ing]
waste[d/ful[ness]]
watch (n.)
watch[dog/
  ful[ness]/man]
water[bottle/fall/
  jug/pipe/proof/
  tight/works/y]
wave[/y]
wax
way[side]

we
weak[en/ness]
wealth[y]
weapon
wear
  (worn-out)
weather
weave[r]
wedding
weed
week[day/end/ly]
weigh[t]
welcome
well (n.)
well[being/born/
  bred/built/
  chosen/deserved/
  meaning/meant]
west[ern]
wet
what
wheat
wheel
when
where
  (also -where, e.g.
  in somewhere)
whether
which
while
whip
whisper
whistle
white[hot/n/ness/
  wash]
who
whole
why
wicked[ness]
wide[awake/n/
  spread/th]
widow[er]
wife
wild
will (n.)
will (v.)
[un] willing[ness]
win
wind (v.)

window
wind[y]
wine
wing
winter[ry/time]
wipe
wire
[un] wise
  (wisdom)
wish
within
with[out]
witness
woman
wonder[ful]
wood[ed/en/land/work]
wool[len]
word
work[day/er/ing[s]/
  ing-class/ing-day/
  ing-man/s/shop]
  ([un]workable)
world[-famous/wide]
worm
worry[/ied/ing]
worship
worth[less]
wound[ed]
wrap[ped/per]
wreck
wrist[-watch]
write[r/ing]
  (written)
wrong[doer/doing]

yard
year[ly]
yellow[ness]
yes
yesterday
yet
yield[ing]
you
young
  (youth[ful])

zero
zoo

Oxford 대학출판부/외국어연수사간 (한국내 판권 : 외국어연수사에서 보유)
ESL/EFL 교재 저술의 세계적 권위 L. H. Hill 박사의 명저

Stories for Reproduction Series 1~4

이야기의 재현(再現)을 통해 배우는 영어 1~4집

■흥미진진한 이야기를 읽거나 듣고 말과 글로 다시 표현해 보는 연습을 통해 표현력(作文・會話)・이해력(讀解・聽解)을 획기적으로 향상시키는 교재

● 이미 40여권의 ESL/EFL(English as a Second/Foreign Language) 교재 저술로 세계적 명성을 떨치고 있는 Leslie A. Hill 박사가 그의 오랜 연구와 교육자로서의 경험을 토대로 최근에 집대성한 영어학습교재의 결정판.

● Hill 박사 특유의 Contextualized Approach(문맥적 접근법)에 토대를 둔 다양한 Oral /Written Reproduction Questions & Exercises(구두/필기재현연습)로 표현력과 이해력의 획기적 향상.

● A. S. Hornby 의 Guide to Patterns & Usage in English(25 구문 유형)에 토대를 두고 단어와 구문의 난이도에 따라 상용 기본단어를 4 단계(입문, 초급, 중급, 상급)로 나누어 익히고 활용시키는 교재 총서.

● 영어 실력이 약한 경우는 기초실력 재확립용으로, 어휘력・문법실력이 앞선 경우는 속독력・청해력・작문력・회화력 향상용으로 쓸 수 있는 교재.

● 교실수업, 자습 양용으로 쓸 수 있으며 자습의 경우를 위해 상세하고 친절한 주석과 해답이 담긴 Study Guide와 Answer Key를 마련.

■대학입시・취직시험・각종고시・TOFEL 등 각종 영어 시험 준비용으로 최적.

제 1 집 　Introductory, Elementary, Intermediate Advanced Stories for Reproduction 1
　　　　전 4권　Textbook＋Study Guide＋Cassette Pack.

제 2 집 　Introductory, Elementary, Intermediate, Advanced Stories for Reproduction 2
　　　　전 4권　Textbook＋Answer Key＋Cassette Pack.

제 3 집 　Introductory, Elementary, Intermediate, Advanced Steps to Understanding
　　　　전 4권　Textbook＋Answer Key＋Cassette Pack.

제 4 집 　Elementary, Intermediate, Advanced Stories for Reproduction, American
　　　　Series 전 3권　Textbook＋Answer Key＋Cassette Pack.

만 화 영 어

만화를 즐기며 연마하는 영어 회화 · 작문 교재

English through Cartoons

Dialogues, Stories & Questions

유우머와 **기지**가 넘치는 **만화**를 즐기면서

(A) **대화**(Dialogues)를 읽거나 테이프를 듣고 영어 특유의
   유우머 감각을 몸에 익히며

(B) 만화를 해설하는 **이야기**(Stories)를 공란을 메우면서 완성하는
   연습을 통해 **작문력**을 기르고

C) 만화내용의 **질의 응답**을 통해 격조 높은 영어 **회화력**을
   양성하는 영작문 · 회화 연습 교재의 결정판!

● EFL/ESL (English as a Foreign/Second Language) 교재 저술의 세계적 권위
 Leslie A. Hill 박사와 세계적인 만화가 **D. Mallet** 의 최신 역작.

● 폭소와 홍소를 자아내게 하면서도 깊은 뜻을 담은 만화와 대화는 학습상의 긴장을
 덜어 주며 Stories 의 공란을 추리하여 완성토록 유도하는 연습문제와 내용 파악
 질의문은 영어의 회화력·청취력·작문력·독해력을 획기적으로 연마·향상.

● 학습 부담을 줄이고 능률을 최대한으로 올리기 위하여 친절하고 자세한 해설과 예문이
 풍부하게 수록된 Study Guide 를 따로 마련.

SMALL TALK
OXFORD UNIVERSITY PRESS 1986.CAROLYN GRAHAM저
Cassette 2개, 교재1권으로 미국영어 특유의 발음을 Jazz Chant로 배우는 최신간

그릇된 발음으로 영어를 배운 기간이 길면 길수록 그것이 영어 청취력과 회화력 향상에 큰 장애가 된다는 것은 ESL/EFL 교사들 모두가 통감하고 있는 사실이다. 이 문제를 근본적으로 해결하려는 시도에서 마련된 것이 이 교재이다.

이 교재는 미국영어의 정확한 발음, 특히 강세(Stress), 음조(Intonation), 음률(Rhythm)과 연음(Blending)및 축약음(Contraction)의 학습에 중점을 두고 있다.

특히 본문의 대화(Dialog)를 Jazz 노래가락으로 만들어 녹음해 놓았기 때문에 노래를 배우듯이 이것을 따라 부르다 보면 자신도 모르게 Native Speaker와 같은 회화력을 습득할 수 있다.

이 교재는 주로 한국어·일본어 등과 같은 **음절어(Syllabic Language)**를 쓰는 국민들이 **음률어(Rhythmic Language)**인 영어의 정확한 발음 특히 음조, 강세, 음률등을 습득하는 데 경이적인 효과를 나타내고 있어 전세계 영어 교육계의 주목을 끌고 있다.

Cassette 1

세계적으로 유명한 Jazz 음악가들이 연주한 Jazz 음악을 배경으로 교재 본문이 노래가락으로 녹음되어 있다.

Cassette 2

Cassette 1의 본문을 응용한 다양한 청취 연습과 Word Puzzle로 된 흥미 진진한 청취 연습 문제가 수록되어 있다.

저자 Carolyn Graham은 New York University의 교수로서 The American Language Institute에서 ESL(English as a second language)을 가르치고 있으며 Jazz를 활용한 Jazz Chants(1978), Jazz Chants for Children(1979), 및 The Electric Elephant(1982)등의 영어회화 교재를 저술한바 있다.

한국내총판 : (주)외국어연수사

단시일내에 미국 본토인의 빠른 대화
청취에 적응할 수 있는 최신
청취력 개발 코오스

Listen for It
Task-based American English Listening Course

영자 신문은 읽을수 있는데, AFKN 방송은 이해가 안가는 분, TOFEL이나 TOEIC의 Listening Comprehension 성적이 향상되지 않는 분, 미국인 교수의 강의를 거의 알아 듣지 못하는 분은 처음부터 이 교재로 빠른 대화 듣기 적응훈련을 받으면 단시일내에 고민이 해결될 것입니다.

고교 상급반이나 대학생들은 선배들의 전철을 밟지 말고 지금부터 이 교재로 청취 훈련을 받으면 선배들처럼 시간을 낭비하지 않고 빠른 시일내에 미국인과의 대화는 물론 미국인 교수의 강의를 들을 수 있는 확고한 기초가 생길 것입니다.

이 교재는 일상적 관심사를 화제(topic)로 삼아 미국인들이 다양한 기능(function)으로 이야기하는 대화에 토대를 두고 있기 때문에 그대로 일상회화에 응용할 수 있습니다.

이 교재는 고등학교 상급반이나 대학 또는 성인영어회화 과정에 적합하도록 다음과 같이 4부로 꾸며져 있습니다.

Starting out : 화재를 소개하고 대화의 배경을 이루는 정보를 제공하며 대화를 이해 하는데 필요한 표현(낱말·숙어 등)을 설명.

Listening for : 화제(topic)와 관련된 몇 가지의 과제 해결에 토대를 둔 청취 활동.

Trying it out : 실제로 회화에 응용해서 말해보는 활동.

이 교재를 자력으로 공부하고자 하는 분들은 녹음대본과 설문의 해답이 수록된 별책 자습서를 이용하면 좋을 것입니다.

총판 : (株)外國語硏修社
서울시 영등포구 여의도동 35-2
백상빌딩 1006호
Tel : 785-0919, 785-1749

교재의 구성 : Student Book : 1권 자습서 : 1권 Tape : C-60 8개

최신간 AMERICAN ENGLISH Course

ON COURSE (1~2권)

© Oxford University Press 1989

■ 2단계로 되어 있는 **On Course**는 초급-중급 수준의 **성인용 영어 회화** 과정으로서 **말하고 듣는** 기능을 중심으로 꾸며진 편리한 교재이다.

■ 학생용 교재는 **30단원**으로 구성되어 있는데 각 단원은 2쪽씩이다. 그래서 사용하기가 아주 편리하며 **50분간**에 학습을 마칠 수 있도록 꾸며져 있다.

■ 또한 학생 상호간의 연습 기회를 제공하기 위하여 두 사람이 **역할놀이**를 하는 것과 빈칸에 알맞는 말을 넣어 대화를 완성하는 **연습문제**가 마련되어 있다.

■ 그리고 5단원씩 묶어서 요약하여 연습하는 총 24쪽의 6개 **요약단원** (Summary Units)이 있는데, 이것들은 30단원에 걸쳐 제시된 재료와 자연스럽게 재 결합하여 이를 보강해 준다.

■ 각 요약 단원마다 **청취력 향상**을 위한 **과제 중심의 연습** 문제가 수록되어 있다.

판매대행 : **(주)외국어연수사**

서울 영등포구 여의도동 35-2
백상빌딩 1006호
☎ 785-0919, 1749, 780-2817

최신간 AMERICAN ENGLISH Course

EAST WEST (1~3권)
© Oxford University Press 1989

3단계 과정(3권)으로 구성된 EAST-WEST는 **중—상급** 수준의 성인용 영어회화 과정으로서 **의사 소통 기능의 향상**을 주목적으로 개발된 것이다. **문법, 기능, 주제, 상황** 등을 골고루 **통합**한 이상적 교수요목(syllabus)에 토대를 두고 있어, 이 교재는, 의사 소통 능력 향상을 위하여 용의 주도하게 통제된 학습 활동을 통하여, **말하고 듣는 연습**을 철저히 할 수 있도록 꾸며져 있다.

특 장

1 모든 영어 회화 교육에 적합하나 특히 말하기를 꺼리는 학생들에게나 학생수가 많은 경우에 크게 도움이 된다.
2 전 교과를 통해서 자연스런 언어를 사용했으나, 이와 다르거나 대안으로 쓰일 표현도 유의 했다.
3 미국 생활의 여러 국면을 소개하기 위해 culture capsules란을 두었다.
4 학생들의 관심을 끌고, 생활 체험을 이용하며, 솔선하여 말을 하도록 유도하는 의사 소통 중심의 교재이다.
5 언어의 내용을 반복하면서 회화력을 육성하는 과정과 과제를 푸는 과정에서 학생들에게 필요한 여러가지 도움을 주고 있다.
6 두 사람이나 소집단의 역할놀이와 빈칸에 적합한 말을 넣는 연습문제들이 광범하게 사용되었다.

단원의 구성

- 총 14단원으로 구성되어 있는 총천연색의 학생용 교재는 각 단원의 8쪽씩으로 되어 있다.
- 각 단원은 각 단원의 교수 요점을 소개하는 대화로 시작된다.
- 다음 4쪽에는 발음 연습을 포함하여 정확성과 유창성의 향상을 노리는 말하는 연습이 따른다.
- 다음에는 문법상의 요점, 상황에 맞는 표현, 기능[목적] 및 개념에 적합한 표현과 각 단원에 쓰인 숙어적 표현등을 요약하는 Checklist란이 있다.
- 마지막 두쪽은 수동적 기능인 청취력과 독해력을 향상시키기 위한 것이다.
- 제1권에는 Moon of India라는 추리 소설을 14편으로 나누어 각 단원마다 실어 독자의 흥미를 유발하고 독서의 즐거움을 맛보게 해 준다.
- East West 는 각 권마다 학생용의 교재 및 연습장, 교사용 교재와 카셋트로 되어 있다. 별도로 Moon of India의 카셋트도 있다.

판매대행 : **(주) 외국어연수사**

서울 영등포구 여의도동 35-2 백상빌딩 1006호
☎ 785-0919, 1749, 780-2817

Common Problems in KOREAN ENGLISH
한국식 영어의 허점과 오류

이 책의 목적은 한국식 영어의 허점과 오류를 바로 잡아주고 「자연스럽고 (natural), 적응성이 풍부하며 (flexible), 관용적인 (idiomatic)」 영어 표현을 익히도록 하려는 것이다. 그러므로 이 책은 영어를 자주 써야하는 분들이나 각급학교 영어선생님들과 올바른 영어 표현을 익히고자 하는 학생들에게 유익한 참고서나 길잡이가 될 것이다.

특 색

- 한국식 영어 특유의 오용 사례를 정선한 후 그 원인을 밝혀내어 상세히 설명하고 올바른 표현법을 구체적으로 예시하였다.
- 오용 사례를 (1) 문법적 오류 (2) 낱말 뜻의 혼동 (3) 어색하거나 부적절한 표현의 3편으로 나누어 그 잘못을 지적하고 올바른 문장으로 고쳐 놓았으며, 그 대안으로 다양한 표현방법을 풍부한 예문으로 제시했을 뿐 아니라 방대한 연습문제를 만들고 그 모범답안까지 제시해 두었다.
- 내용설명은 물론 예문과 대화례 (sample sentences and dialogs) 등이 저자 특유의 간명한 필치로 씌어져 있어 이해하기 쉽고 활용도 용이하다.
- 각 문제점의 요점을 간추려 우리말로 옮겨 놓았으며 교실 수업과 자습 양용에 적합하도록 만들었다.

저 자

David Kosofsky는 The University of Maryland에서 서양사를 전공했고 (B.A.) Brandeis University에서 비교 역사학을 전공했으며 (M.A.) 미국, 일본 및 말레이지아에서 영어를 가르쳤고 1982년에 내한한 이래 서강대학교 영어교육연구소에서 Advanced Seminar class를 가르치면서 영어학습교재의 연구개발에 전념하고 있다. 그는 The Asian Wall Street Journal과 Asiaweek에 기고하면서 소설도 써 왔다.

주석 · 증보판

PRACTICE WITH IDIOMS
영어 숙어 연습

Ronald E. Feare ● 李 澄 載 譯編

〈특 장〉

◉ 영어 숙어의 뜻과 구문 지식을 체계적으로 습득하기 위한 중-상급 수준의 영어 학습 교재이다.

◉ 복잡 다단한 영어 숙어를 16종의 구문 유형으로 분류하고 각 유형에 속하는 숙어로 연습문제를 구성하여 그것들을 문맥적으로 이해하는 과정에 학습자를 참여시킨 다음 숙어의 정의(定義), 연어법(連語法) 및 예문(例文)을 소개하는 귀납적 문제 해결 방법으로 꾸며놓았다.

◉ 각 장의 「숙어의 해설(Explanation of the Idioms)」항에는 숙어의 정의(Definition)」와 연어법(Collocation) 그리고 예문(Sample Sentences)이 수록되어 있는데, 이 한국어 주석·증보판에서는 이것들을 대폭 증보한 후 그 번역과 주석을 붙여 놓아 영어 실력이 약한 중급 수준 이하의 학습자에게도 도움이 되도록 배려하였다.

◉ 제17장 부록에는 숙어의 이해에 필요한 문법용어의 설명과 16종의 숙어 구문형을 도해와 예문을 통해 일목요연하게 설명하는 동시에 그 용법에 대한 유의 사항도 덧붙여 놓았는데, 이 장은 전문이 한국어로 번역되어 있다.

◉ 각장의 연습문제에 대한 해답을 제시하고, 이 책에서 다룬 숙어들의 적절한 예문들을 각종 문헌과 사전들에서 골라 한국어 번역문과 주석을 붙여 별책으로 꾸며놓았다.

연락처 \ 한국내 판권보유 : (주) 외국어연수사

서울特別市 永登浦區 汝矣島洞35-2 (白象빌딩1006號) ☎ 785-0919. 785-1749

미국 영어회화의 최고봉을 정복하는
OXFORD AMERICAN ENGLISH COURSE

JACK C. RICHARDS DAVID BYCINA

PERSON TO PERSON
Communicative Speaking and Listening Skills

© Oxford University Press, Book 1, 1984; Book 2, 1985

교재 구성 : Book1 : Student Book 1권, 자습서 1권, 테잎 6개
　　　　　 Book2 : Student Book 1권, 자습서 1권, 테잎 6개

1 OXFORD가 특별히 한국과 일본 영어학도들의 취약점을 연구한 끝에 Communicative Speaking & Listening Skills 연마에 역점을 두고 개발한 Best Seller로 大學生/ 一般成人用의 영어회화 최종완성 Course.

2 각 Unit마다 1. Presentation Dialogue〔대화〕 2. Give It A Try〔연습〕 3. Listen to This〔청취〕로 나누어, 전 30 Units에 걸쳐 110종의 다양한 Topics를 148 종의 Communicative Function으로 엮은 Functional Course의 결정판.

3 Stress(강세), Intonation(음조) 및 Rhythm(음률) 등 초분절음소의 철저한 학습과 Communicative Skills 습득에 필수적인 특수 구문 및 어법의 집중 훈련에 주안점을 둔 새로운 교재.

4 실용/학술의 각국면을 생생하게 연출하여 12개의 Cassette에 압축한 입체음향 교재로 Communicative Speaking은 물론, Tasks, Note—taking, Gap—filling, Dialogue Completion 및 Multiple Choice 등의 연습을 통하여 구미 유학에 지장이 없는 청취력을 양성하는 Course로 TOEFL, 취직시험 등 각종 영어시험 대비용으로도 최적.

연락처╲ 한국내 총판 : (주) 외국어연수사

서울特別市 永登浦區 汝矣島洞 35-2(白象빌딩 1006號) ☎ 785-0919. 785-1749

저자소개

L. A. Hill 박사는 ELT (English Language Teaching)
교재의 저술가로서 그리고 영어 교육계의 세계적인
권위자로 널리 알려진 분으로 그의 저서에는 다음과 같은
것들이 있다.
Stories for Reproduction 1 (전 4 권), Stories for
Reproduction 2 (전 4 권), Stories for Reproduction:
American Series (전 3 권), Steps to Understanding
(전 4 권), Word Power 1500/3000/4500 (전 3 권),
English through Cartoons (전 2 권), Elementary &
Intermediate Composition Pieces (전 2 권), Elementary &
Intermediate Comprehension Pieces (전 2 권),
Intermediate Comprehension Topics, Oxford Graded
Readers (전 4 권), Writing for a Purpose, Note-taking
Practice, A Guide to Correct English & Exercises
(전 2 권), Prepositions & Adverbial Particles &
Exercises (전 2 권), Contextualized Vocabulary Tests
(전 4 권), Crossword Puzzle Book (전 4 권).

Advanced Stories for Reproduction 1

1985년   2월 5일   인쇄
1985년   2월 12일   발행

판권본사소유

지은이   L. A. HILL
펴낸이   李 瀅 載
펴낸곳   外國語研修社
서울 • 영등포구 여의도동 35-2
등록   1977. 5. 18. 제10-81호
전화   785-0919, 1749
FAX : 780-2817